74

Every Song
Tells A Story

A Brief History of Popular Music

To John,
All the best
Mike

Mike Hurst

ISBN 978-09553648 6 0
ISBN 09553648 6 8

Published by
Polperro Heritage Press,
Clifton-upon-Teme, Worcestershire WR6 6EN UK
www.polperropress.co.uk

Cover design
Steve Bowgen

Printed by
Cromwell Press
Trowbridge, Wiltshire
United Kingdom

Contents

To all the great musicians and songwriters I have ever known... and the countless others I wish I had!

Preface

It seems to me I have spent nearly all my life in the music business. Actually I have, albeit the first 14 as a child performer. An old fashioned term for this was 'a speciality act', which invariably did not mean an extraordinary talent, rather, as in my case, simply a small somewhat precocious child singing *California Here I Come* at a London Variety theatre. The reason for this was that my mother ran a children's theatre group, so it was as natural for me to take to the stage as it would have been for others to take up football or cricket, though perhaps not quite as healthy!

It also meant I was exposed to music of all kinds from an early age. A Radio Rentals wireless gave me access to American Forces Network, AFN, where I not only heard all the great Irving Berlin and Cole Porter songs, but also something that would be classified today as 'alternative', Louis Jordan's Rhythm & Blues and Hank Williams's Country music.

These formative beginnings established my love, and I mean love, of popular music. I was taken to the London Palladium in 1947 to see Frank Sinatra. I got to meet early 1950s British stars like Dickie Valentine and Ronnie Hilton, and I met Buddy Holly in 1958. Oh, and I sang at the premiere of *Jailhouse Rock* at the Empire, Leicester Square. How lucky can one boy get? I knew one day I would be part of this exciting business... my mother told me, so it was bound to happen. Like most mothers, she was right. Well, eventually.

I had to have a 'proper job' first, so I did what all other aspiring music wannabees did; I joined Lloyd's of London as a trainee broker in 1961. I hated every minute of it, mainly because I had no idea what I was supposed to be doing. The billiards hall in Lime Street, London held a greater attraction, as did the Grapes public house in Fenchurch Street. However, I got a break when my mother answered an ad in *The Stage* newspaper on my behalf for a 'young singer/guitarist'. I auditioned and to my utter joy, not to mention amazement, got the 'gig'. I became one of the Springfield Trio, alongside Dusty and her brother Tom. Within a few weeks our record of *Silver Threads and Golden Needles* was in the American Top 10, and I was in Nashville, Tennessee. We were the first British vocal group, ever, to have a hit in the USA, and we became the top group in the UK that same year, 1962.

After the group's demise, I ran my own band with Jimmy Page, Albert Lee, and Tony Ashton. I also sang with Phil Everly, albeit for a fortnight! Then in 1964 I hosted the first teen show on BBC radio. On the programme, imaginatively called *Teen Scene*, I interviewed most of 'Swinging London', from Michael Caine to Jean Shrimpton and Bob Dylan.

In 1965 I stopped messing around and became a record producer. I got lucky: I found Marc Bolan and Cat Stevens. From then on the 1960s were really swinging, for me as well as everyone else under 30.

Hit after hit with Cat, Manfred Mann, PP Arnold, Spencer Davis and The Move made me top UK producer in 1967. But Woodstock in 1969 somehow told me the writing was on the wall for the coming decade. Middle-aged hippy lawyers puffing spliffs the size of Cumberland sausages were everywhere. Accountants were throwing away the three-piece suits, swapping them for open neck shirts and flares, and running record companies; shock horror! Even worse, lawyers began to think they could pick hit records. What had the world come to?

Through the 1970s I produced a never ending stream of hits for Showaddywaddy, and the same for Shakin' Stevens in the 1980s. But in 1989 I experienced a revelation; after 30 years there might be something else other than making records, especially as the record companies made it plain I was past my 'sell by' date. This despite 52 Top 40 records, two number ones, 25 gold and platinum albums, all totalling around 40 million sales!

I am and have always been a history 'buff'. I love facts, dates and trivia; from Wild Bill Hickock's cards when he was in shot in the back by Charlie McCall which became known as the 'deadman's hand', right through to the history of firearms from matchlocks to cartridge. I amass information; pretty useless unless you happen to be someone with an irritating cough on *Who Wants To Be A Millionaire?* - or unless you want to write a book.

I was commissioned to do just that in 1989, a book on the history of popular music. I worked hard, came up with reams of research, and then the company went bust. As you do, I shoved a years worth of work in a drawer and forgot about it. Then in 1994 I was asked to give a talk at my son's school on 'my life in music'. Realising they would probably be bored by an old fart recounting his memories, I decided to make use of the 'stuff in the drawer'.

My talk on the history of English-speaking popular music, called The Musikmakers, has since become a firm favourite with schools up and down the country. I actually give around 50 lectures annually, to a total of about 4,000 sixth formers. It has been a huge success, so much so that Heads and General Studies Directors have constantly asked when I am going to write 'the' book.

In 2000, I put together a website called the musikmakers.com. With the help of four researchers, I amassed even more information than I had originally, and the site got over 5,000 hits per day (and subsequently went bust!). It was then that I realised there was <u>no</u> book on the history of popular music. There were plenty on jazz, on blues, on rock, but not one which traced the disparate strands of all English speaking pop from the earliest times.

So, here we are. My love for music and my involvement with it for over 50 years has finally resulted in an attack of self-discipline, and this book.

I hope you are sitting comfortably.

Mike Hurst
2008

Introduction

There has always been music: there will always be music. It is with us from the cradle to the grave. Mothers sing nursery rhymes to us, we form our adolescent ideas through pop lyrics, we fall in love to music and even in death there is still music even though we don't hear it (allegedly). It is an eternal theme.

Perhaps Neolithic man found the rib cage of a mammoth made a great xylophone, by accident naturally, or the stretched skin of a sabre tooth tiger made an excellent percussive sound.

This is conjecture, but the use of the human voice throughout history and pre-history is not; warcries to terrify enemies; soothing sounds to keep the children happy, and songs of worship in any creed. Music is love and above all the voice of the people throughout time.

But what is 'popular music'? By definition it is that music enjoyed by the largest number of people at any given moment in time. It cannot therefore be elitist, as was classical music. I say 'was' because now classical music, or much of it, is certainly popular. Both time and technology have put it in the mainstream. However, it has always lacked that all important ingredient, lyrics.

Pop is words and music. It is not high art, and it often borders on the banal. Quality is not always a guarantee of success and why should it be?

Pop is an art form seen as trivial by some, but equally regarded by many as an important cultural development, the voice of history. All societies have their legends and myths, handed down by word of mouth. The written word is mighty, but music with words can be even stronger, bearing in mind more people on this earth listen rather than read, and have done throughout history.

A 16th century quotation reads:
'if a man were permitted to make the ballads of a nation, he need not care who should make its laws'.

I have no idea who was responsible for these words, but that does not matter. Their meaning is clear: musical composers have always been the unconscious law givers and moulders of national moods and aspirations. We only know those of our own generation and perhaps some from recent history, but the history of civilisation is like a tree: its roots are deep in the ground thus we tend to be ignorant of the source of its fruit.

The Ancient Greeks deified music, ranking it higher than drama and poetry. Aristotle put it perfectly:

To reform or to relax the manners of a people it suffices to add a string to the lyre or to take one from it.

… a pattern for popular music that remains dominant to this day.

In the West the early voices are all but lost to us. Wealth, education, and sophistication have relegated our oral traditions to the borders of absurdity for many. The young find 'folk evenings' at the pub derisory. They laugh at the imagery of people in fishing jumpers and bushy orange beards singing in a keening, nasal whine about days gone by. What a pity, and what a mistake. You see, the most potent force in the world's music industry today is largely based on one thing - the English language - and it has been that way for nearly 200 years. World Music?

This is a 'catch all' for many ethnic music forms desperate for recognition outside their recognised borders, and for record companies desperate for sales. Sometimes that works, especially the Latino influences, but on a minor level. Just as the world has chosen English as the first tongue of the emergency airwaves, air and sea communication, so it is with entertainment. In the 20th century this was due almost entirely to America, but this story goes back much further.

1

Early Notes

The story of King Arthur is a myth, created by Geoffrey of Monmouth and translated by Mallory in the Middle Ages. But we <u>now</u> know there was a tribal chieftain called Arthur, and, more interestingly, there was a Druid, Merlin. These people were Celts and in the 6th century they were about to be swept away by the invading Saxon hordes from mainland Northern Europe.

An acolyte of Merlin was a young man called Taliesin. History has it that his voice was flawless, and possessed magical qualities. We must take history's word for it as we have no record of his melodies. What we do have are his words handed down to us through time in The Song Of Taliesin; they capture more succinctly than most modern day writers the true essence of the songwriter:

> *I am the singer,*
> *And I am the song,*
> *And I hold these things in trust.*

Those words come to us from the past, nearly 1500 years ago. The name of Taliesin also appears to hold a fascination for many in recent history. Deep Purple recorded an album entitled *The Book of Taliesin*: Roald Dahl's version of *Snow White* was set to music, performed by the Taliesin Orchestra. I wonder if the names of Elvis, Sinatra and the Beatles, not to mention their music, will resonate in 3000 AD? Taliesin and other Celtic bards can have had no idea what they were starting. Their influence can be heard in the traditional sounds of the British and Irish folk song and its hugely successful progeny, American Country Music.

But Celtic was destined to become a minority tongue, pushed to the fringes of North Western Europe. In Britain it was to be absorbed by another far more potent language, Anglo-Saxon. I say 'absorbed' rather than 'destroyed' because that would turn out to be the abiding strength of 'Old/New English'. Just as 19th century American immigrants from all corners of the globe influenced the English language, so it was in Britain between 500 and 1300 AD, culminating in English becoming the world language in the present day. I am convinced it will continue to be so for one reason: it is the only expanding language on earth, drawing its richness and diversity from a multitude of cultures. Therefore, in one real sense, pop can be seen as a predominantly English language inspiration. For further proof take note of the closing paragraphs of this chapter.

Before I am accused of bias and even xenophobia, let me try and put this in a musical context. A 'melting pot' of racial groups in the USA during the 18th and 19th centuries gave birth to Ragtime, Blues, Jazz and Rock n' Roll, but during the first 1000 years AD, it was a similar influence of Roman, Celt, Saxon, Dane, Viking and Norman in the British Isles that set the pattern of what was to follow.

Popular music was inspired by warfare, love and tales of adventure. As the Saxon settlers swept across Britain, the retreating Celts attempted to stem the tide. Painted in woad and brandishing their war axes, they would sing (scream!) battle songs like *Bali Mawr*, specifically designed to strike fear into the hearts of their foe. The music was designed to shock as it often had been, from Joshua's trumpets at Jericho to the *Ride of The Valkyries* in the movie *Apocalypse Now*. Put into a more contemporary context, much of present day pop has been known to shock, from the raucous sounds of James Brown and Little Richard through to the anarchistic Punk movement and thus to the present day 'club' sounds, the only difference being those on the receiving end, the 'enemy', the older generation!

By 610 AD the Celts had been pushed to the fringes of Britain, and England had become a country of Saxon kingdoms. Within 100 years they had become Christian, though hedging their bets and allowing paganism to flourish alongside this new religion.

12

An interesting development in choral music took place in 778 AD, when a new form of liturgical chant became popular in Switzerland, or what passed for Switzerland at that time. The Gregorian Chant, named after Pope Gregory, is still a mainstay of the Catholic Church today, and has also influenced pop vocal groups and backing singers. It's good to know the Swiss have a cultural claim to fame other than the cuckoo clock and the gnomes of Zurich.

In the 9th century, King Alfred the Great revived literacy and learning. He was the only English king to write books before Henry VIII, which included translating the Anglo Saxon Chronicles and he allowed writing to flourish in the Christian church. We know he was a dreadful cook, but we have no idea if he loved music. However, the echoes of the Chronicles can be heard in the Heavy Metal bands of the 1970s and 80s. Groups like Iron Maiden and the appropriately named Saxon, even looked like their forebears with their long unkempt hair and amulets. You can even picture them on the battle line at Edington in 878 AD, where Arthur defeated the Danes. I am sure they would have put the fear of God into them, singing *Bring Your Daughter To The Slaughter*!

The Viking invasions of England in the 9th and 10th centuries brought yet another cultural dimension with their Norse Sagas. The most famous of these was *Beowulf*, a poem of truly epic proportion. It would be almost 1000 years before another 'Viking' invasion conquered the music world, with Abba in the 1970's, but then they were singing in English.

The first 'recorded' song on British soil was heard in 1066, October 14 to be precise... and, shock horror, it was in French! When William the Bastard lined up his Normans at the foot of Senlac Hill, Hastings, his troubadour/minstrel Taillefer, asked for the honour of charging the Saxon lines first. History does not relate if William was a music lover, but it looks unlikely as he gave his servant permission to die. Taillefer charged the English, throwing his lance in the air and <u>singing</u>. He sang *The Song Of Roland*, an epic glorifying one of Charlemagne's great generals.

Quite obviously the English were not music lovers either and they hated the Normans . The latter was more likely, but the result was the same. They cut poor Taillefer to pieces - the first time a musician is known to have died at an English seaside resort. They have been doing so ever since, mostly on Saturday nights at the local ballroom.

The Norman invasion marked the last time England was invaded, and the last time a foreign culture made a significant contribution to English life until the 20th century.

At this point I feel the reader may be confused by the reference to Taillefer being a troubadour and a minstrel. There is a very clear distinction between the two. During the reign of Henry II in the mid 12th century, his Queen, Eleanor, became the doyenne of upper class music lovers. She was the first great patron of musical art, although not in England but in Aquitaine where she spent most of her time. She paid handsomely for her troubadours to write songs of courtly love. Written exclusively in French and Latin, this was music of privilege. The 'common' music, the folk music, was written and performed by minstrels, the 'Bob Dylans' of their day, who sang love songs and protest songs in the village and town squares. This was popular music, and most of it was in the language of the common people: English.

The English people after 1066 were a sorry bunch. They had been conquered, had their land stripped from them and their language usurped by a 'ghastly, gutteral tongue', Norman French.

Add to that the sole use of Latin in the churches, and you will realise how impoverished it must have felt to be English. All the more remarkable then, that within 250 years of the Norman invasion, the invaders would themselves be consumed by the language of their serfs, English:

They can take my life but they will never take my freedom
(apologies to Mel Gibson, and all Scots)

To return to my point that the French invaders were a little bankrupt in the musical department, it is also worth recounting the sorry tale of Richard I and his minstrel Blondel. When Richard was captured and held to ransom by a jealous Frankish prince, Blondel set out on a European tour to find his master. His 'one night stands' consisted of standing beneath various castle walls and singing, in

French. One can only imagine the abuse not to mention detritus that must have been thrown his way. However, it worked. At one particular venue, Richard heard his valiant minstrel, gave a signal, and Blondel returned hot foot to England, eager to give the joyous news to Richard's brother John, England's Regent. John, being extremely jealous of his brother and quite happy with the trappings of royalty, promptly put Blondel to death. No, life was still less than perfect for a musician in Norman England.

But their songs were alive and well. So well in fact, that around 1260, a song was written that remains today as probably the oldest folk song still in existence on the planet, more or less in its original form! The song is called *Summer Is A Coming In*, or in old English, *Sumer Is Icumen In*.

Now think about that. Prior to 1260 we have no knowledge of the notation of any popular songs, anywhere. *Sumer Is Icumen In* was written, allegedly, in Reading, possibly by the monks at the Abbey. We will never know the composer, but we should be grateful for his gift.

> *Sumer is icumen in*
> *Loudly sing cuckoo*
> *Sumer is icumen in*
> *Loudly sing cuckoo.*

By the end of the 100 Years War, the Norman ruling class became convinced that they were much better of on their tiny island, set apart from the Europeans and their troubles, and what better way of establishing their individuality than by adopting an alien tongue, English.

Henry IV was the first monarch to address his Parliament in its native language in 1399. Religion followed suit with the advent of Anglicism in the person of John Wycliffe and the Lollards. But it was the literary revolution of Geoffrey Chaucer that finally gave the English a common voice:

> '*Common English that is spoken in one shire varieth from another, but by using English not over rude, nor curious, but in such terms as shall be understood by God's grace, most people will understand*'.
> Chaucer.

By 1476 William Caxton had ensured the growth of English with his printing press. All forms of art, including music, could now flourish and develop on a much broader canvas. So, the true beginnings of the rise of popular music can be found as we enter 16th century, in a country that was at ease with itself in speech and literature.

From the mists of Avalon to the strumming of lutes in banqueting halls, the people's music of England would now find its way across oceans and continents. It would be a fitting legacy for Taliesin and Taillefer.

2

A Wandering Minstrel

Computers or rather their 'slaves' have suggested that given the number of notes in our musical scale, all original melodies had been written and used up by the 13th century. How fortunate then that recorded sound, radio and television were not on the horizon and even musical notation was still in its infancy. This meant that in the Middle Ages, no one was aware of plagiarism or if they were they did not give a hoot. After all, it must have been a blessed time around 1500; there were no lawyers.

The 16th century was the Golden Age of the minstrel, and the popular song was even in evidence in royal circles.

Henry VIII was no mean songwriter. He wrote of love and rejection, and let's face it, he knew all about the latter: he invented the word. He is credited by some with writing one of the greatest love songs of all, *Greensleeves*. It is said he wrote it for Anne Boleyn, whom he loved madly, but there is no absolute provenance. What is indisputable is the song's fantastic longevity. Shakespeare mentions it three times in his *Merry Wives of Windsor*, which perhaps is one reason for it being attributed to Henry:

> *But they do no more adhere and keep place together than the Hundreth Psalm to the tune of Greensleeves*
> Act 2, Scene 1, Merry Wives Of Windsor

It was given new words in the late 19th century by William Chatterton Dix, retitled *What Child Is This?*, and last entered the Top 20 in the 1950s! It is the longest running hit of all time and surely eclipses *The Sound Of Music* on those grounds alone. However, it is a rather wimpy, limp little number, not to everyone's taste.

I think the first truly great English love song was *Barbara Allen*. The Scots claim this too, so I will not be dogmatic: let's share it. Certainly the strength of the tune was such that within a few years there were at least 28 versions spread around Europe in as many languages. This was surely the first Eurovision hit. On January 2, 1666, the diarist Samuel Pepys remarks on a tremendous performance of the song by the emotional actress Mrs Knipp at a soiree given by Lord Brounker at his London mansion.

The lyric is literally to die for:

> *In Scarlet Town where I was born*
> *There was a young maid dwelling,*
> *And all the boys cried lack a day*
> *For love of Barbara Allen*
>
> *Twas in the merry month of May*
> *When green buds were a'swelling,*
> *Young Jemmy Grove on his death bed lay,*
> *For love of Barbara Allen.*

What a story. Boy meets girl: boy falls in love with girl: girl rejects boy: boy dies! The lyric is forever, and it has become the staple diet of lyricists ever since. Think *Oh Carol* by Neil Sedaka in 1961:

> *Oh Carol, I am but a fool,*
> *Darling I love you though you treat me cruel.*
> *You hurt me, and you make me cry,*
> *But if you leave me, I will surely die.*

You see? As most working songwriters say, once you've hit on a great formula, don't mess with it. *Barbara Allen* is probably the template for all love songs in the English language thereafter.

Talking of formulas, Rowan Atkinson and Richard Curtis certainly hit on one with their *Blackadder* television series. But did they know how close they were to the truth in the Elizabethan programmes? Good Queen Bess is portrayed as a 'nut', but in truth she had certain bizarre traits. One was that she called her courtiers and herself by animal names, inspired by a Scottish 'broadsong', *Mr Frog Wuld Cum To The Old Myl Dur*. Sir Francis Drake became Dick the Drake. She herself was Miss Mouse, and the French Duke d'Alencon, an ambassador and erstwhile suitor, was so ugly that Elizabeth thought he looked like a frog: and that is why we call the French 'frogs'. There is a great example of biting political commentary in a pop song from the 16th century. The song lived on to become *Froggie Went A' Courting* in the Appalachian Mountains of America 100 years later, carried there, like so much of our native music, by the first English settlers.

These tales were part of the singing heritage brought to the New World by the English, Scotch, Irish and Welsh.
Burl Ives, 1963

Although, as Ives said, most folk songs are anonymous, many of these 'folk' tunes originated on stage and their provenance is known. The great Shakespearean actor Edmund Keane wrote the words to a traditional English melody, *Sweet Kitty Clover*:

> *Sweet Kitty Clover, she bothers me so*
> *Sing wack fal de dee, sing wack fal de do*
> *Where sweet Kitty lives, I am bound to go*
> *Sing wack fal de dee, sing wack fal de do*

I can visualise my readers thinking that for a Shakespearean actor, Kean was less than erudite. But hold on: this was just pop music.

It acquires the name of folk by its popularity and by the fact that over the years singers add or subtract with freedom from the original.
Burl Ives.

So folk music was pop in its day, plain and simple with no pretensions. For 'wack fal de dee' in the 16th century, read 'A wop ba balooma a wop bam boom' by Little Richard in the 20th. Some things never change.

Look at the song written to commemorate the great fair on August 15th each year at Scarborough. Not only was it revitalised by Simon and Garfunkel in the 20th century, it was also neatly re-written in a major key by Bob Dylan with his *Girl From The North Country*. It's all a bit like Chinese whispers. Lyrics and melodies change from minstrel to minstrel, to suit the time and demonstrate the richness and diversity of the popular song.

We cannot leave the Tudor era without remarking on two further influences on both words and music. Firstly the great writer and poet Edmund Spenser had re-discovered the prosody of Geoffrey Chaucer.

Simply put, this means the ability to bring verse alive through judicious use of vowels and rhyme. Why I mention this is the effect it would have on lyrics of songs from then on. *The Shepherd's Calendar* may be a poem, but you can see how easily it could be sung:

> *Colin, to hear thy rymes and roundelays*
> *Which thou wert wont on wastfull hylls to sing,*
> *I more delight then larke in sommer days;*
> *Whose Echo made the neyghbour groves to ring,*
> *And taught the byrds, which in the lower Spring*
> *Did shroude in shady leaves from sonny rayes,*
> *Frame to thy songe their cheerful cheriping,*
> *Or hold theyr peace, for shame of thy swete layes.*
>
> Edmund Spencer, 1579

Secondly, I have referred previously to privileged music as opposed to music of the people, but now added to the latter I must include religious songs. The composers may well have been subsidised, but their music was available to all. The 16th century is rich in such composers. Thomas Tallis is rightly called the 'Father of English Cathedral music'. Born in Waltham Abbey near London in 1515, he composed many melodies which still survive today. His greatest achievement however, was to nurture the talents of the man who became the most enduring Elizabethan composer of all, William Byrd. Byrd became the honorary organist alongside Tallis at the Chapel Royal in Windsor, but they were both penniless. Elizabeth I gave them both the sole rights to publish and print music in England. Eat your heart out Paul McCartney. But the sad thing was that music was not a business at that time, and they made no money! William Byrd however, left us with a lifetime of marvellous songs, and was the greatest of our old composers, and surely an inspiration for those legends of the 18th century, Johann Sebastian Bach, and England's adopted son George Frederick Handel.

In summarizing this chapter, the reader might be excused for thinking me Anglo-centric. Surely there were folk songs and musicians from other European countries influencing English writers? Of course, music knows no boundaries, and has no constraints. However, this book is concerned with the influence of the English language on music. It is self-evident that as our tongue has become the 'lingua franca' of the world, so has the music or rather, the words. Take *Morning Has Broken* (Russian) or *I Who Have Nothing* (Italian), or a thousand others. In most cases it is the English lyric that has 'sold' the song around the world, with a few exceptions. Melodies are international, they need no translation, but when lyrics are attached, to succeed they generally have to be English, and the roots of this 'fait accompli' can be found in the 16th century.

3

A Brave New World

Since singing is so good a thing,
I wish all men would learn to sing.

These are the words of William Byrd in 1600, a man at the top of his profession. Along with his contemporaries John Bull and Orlando Gibbons, he pioneered the use of rhythm and harmony as set against the old established plainsong. The lute was the instrument of the minstrel, but with the advent of the virginal, the grandfather of the piano, Byrd's possibilities were expanded musically and creatively. In 1611, Byrd and his friends produced the first English book of printed music. Entitled *Parthenia* (The First Book Of Virginals Music), it contained 21 of their compositions, and was presented to Elizabeth, the daughter of James I.

Before returning to the 'true' music of the common man, I must make mention of one other great English composer. Henry Purcell, another Chapel Royal acolyte, had written the music to Macbeth (yes, he was the first Andrew Lloyd Webber) at the age of 14! However, the most interesting part of his career for me, was the accolade given to him by an unknown critic:

He can compose a song in five minutes, and the song lives.

The essence of the 20th century pop writer is condensed into that one line more neatly than any other, but the development of popular music would come from 3,000 miles away, in a New World.

The Southern Appalachians are the mountains where British Folk music became American Folk Heritage during the next two centuries. This occurred for a variety of reasons: the songs could only develop in splendid isolation in the American wilderness: the Puritans were active in both England and the New World, but in England it was an easier task for them to control the public's desire to sing, than in the wilds of a new land. Burl Ives, one of the last great American folk archivists, always recognised where the origins of his country's musical heritage lay:

The ballad is one of the most effective forms of storytelling. It uses vivid images and the most simple statements to express the highlights of a tale, supplementing these with rhythm and music. The most potent of these stories are of unknown authorship, originating at a time when they were not written down. Considering that they were preserved by memory, it is noteworthy that they not only kept intact their power as stories, but also the phrases by which the stories carried their punch.

Burl Ives

Story telling was 'preserved by memory' in many countries and continents, but one continent in particular would have a lasting effect on both music and racial differences, Africa.

There came in a Dutch man-of warre that sold us 20 negars.

These were the words of John Rolfe, a Virginia settler in 1619. They marked the beginning of the Atlantic slave trade and sowed the seeds of a Civil Rights march that would take 350 years, which in the process would give a diversity and excitement to popular music from Spirituals to Rap and Hip-Hop.

In fact these first poor souls were indentured servants not slaves. They would serve a term of five years and then have their freedom. Similar 'arrangements' were also made with impoverished white folk. By any other name it was still a form of slavery.

The Spanish had been importing West African slaves to their New World colonies since 1510, a fact that has been either lost or ignored in the passage of time, as has the unpalatable truth that the providers were more often than not either Arab or black themselves.

But what does all this have to do with music? When completely diverse cultures collide within a common space, the national identity of the weakest is generally subjugated by the strongest.

The African Americans are as confused about their origins as the English appear to be today, and that is because we have all been consumed by an American popular culture. The dreaded political correctness is also at work, endlessly feeding us misconceptions about this and that.

Popular music is no exception. The popular belief is that black Africans arrived in the New World complete with all the requisite parts of Blues, Jazz, Rock and Roll et al, built in. That is obviously not the case, even though in rhythmic terms black African influence has been immense. But do we hear any African folk melodies from the 16th century that contain many other root elements of these music forms? No, because most of the black influences of the last 150 years are African/American as distinct from African. In African tribal culture, songs were composed for the moment and were purely aural as there were no written languages. After a hunt or during ceremonial occasions, someone would write a song commemorating that event, everyone would learn it and sing it, but the next morning it was forgotten and they moved on to the next one. This is pure pop, and completely unlike western Europeans who cherished their musical heritage. But British Folk Heritage has been appropriated by the Americans. Now it is simply categorised as American Heritage music. In Britain we have all but forgotten the 'old' songs'. The younger generation are not aware of them at all!

Traditional British songs are no longer taught in schools and any whiff of traditional folk is seen as cause for ridicule by the young, for whom cool, an American invention, is everything. As far as music is concerned, we appear to have been responsible for little or nothing until the Beatles and the 1960s. Let's get it straight; the English gave their language and folk songs to popular music. You can still hear it today in the melodies and lyrics of Nashville musicians, with Celtic pipes and fiddles. You can hear it in the songs of Woody Guthrie, Bob Dylan, Martin and Liza Carthy, and many others.

But what about Africa's musical heritage? Does it exist? Of course it does, but the African's initial contribution to popular music was a sound: the sound of Africa and it was pop in the very essence of the word. Black Africans employ polyrhythms in their singing. These are rhythmic notes which embellish a melody, and admittedly can be heard in other racial music from Middle Eastern prayer, to European folk songs of the past, but have become the preserve of black American soul singers. Many white artists today attempt to emulate them. Some are extremely successful like Joss Stone and Dusty Springfield, but most are poor imitators who appear unable or unwilling to be themselves.

'Call and response' also features hugely in African culture and is an integral part of the oral traditions of tribal history. This 'sound' is an integral part of the oral traditions of tribal history. Many African tribes have a 'Praise Giver', an early form of PR man, whose duty was to extol the virtues and great deeds of his chief. Shaka, founder of the Zulu Empire, used these 'spin doctors' to great effect. With the whole tribe assembled and the chief waiting to make his grand entrance, the Praise Giver would leap out and shout his ritual praises... 'Our Chief is the mightiest in the land', 'The Great Elephant has 200 wives and 400 children', 'He is the mighty Slayer of Ten Thousand'. In answer to each exhortation, the tribe would chorus 'Yebo Kosi nKosi' (yes, Lord of Lords), 'Si Gi Di!' (slayer of 10,000). Tribal anthropologists refer to this as 'call and response', the echoes of which can be heard in the 'field hollers' of the plantations of the Deep South, and thence to the Blues, Gospel and other 20th century music styles.

There was, of course, a white 'call and response' equivalent. Actually there always had been, in religious services, but another appeared in the 17th century, the sea shanty. The shanty, a corruption of the French verb 'chanter' (to sing), was sung by sailors to help get through the tedium of their daily chores. The Bosun's mate would sing the first line and the crew would follow with an answer:

> Come all ye young fellows that follow the sea
> To my way, hay, blow the man down
> Sea shanty, *Blow The Man Down*

Furthermore, the shuffling dances of much of tribal Africa were also mirrored by the sailors dance, the hornpipe. Not having any room for jigs and reels, the men developed a shuffling dance, in line, to whistle and fiddle accompaniment, not dissimilar to the line dancing of the 20th century in Nashville. Perhaps it is worth mentioning here that many forms of 20th century popular dancing owe much to the county of Yorkshire! The clog dancing from that particular area of England contributed to tap dancing as surely as any African based influence.

Religion played a major part in the growth of popular music. In the early 17th century, Puritanism denied people the right to enjoy themselves through music or any other means. Silent obedience and fear were both its strengths and its weaknesses. A 16th century French theologian, John Calvin, had set in train a new movement with radical ideas which were adopted by non- Lutheran reformed churches. Its basic teaching was the 'absolute sovereignty of the divine will', predestination, and the impossibility of grace, once given, being lost. It also taught that the authority of the Scripture is made known to the believer by the 'internal witness of the Holy Spirit' and that the Sacraments are 'declaratory of grace imparted', but do not themselves convey it. Simply put this is individualism rather than collectivism, and it helped to establish an Evangelical movement which John Wesley propagated through the 18th century and which gave birth to Methodism. Methodists believe in personal conversion and the priesthood for all believers, and its most influential branch in America was the Methodist Episcopal Church.

What does all this have to do with the black African slave? It meant that they could now be accepted into the Christian church, and indeed were seen as 'targets' for conversion by the Evangelists. This new religious movement found its voice in hymns of salvation and glory, which sometimes contained very similar 'call and response' patterns the Africans were accustomed to. In Britain natural conservatism muted the evangelical fervour, but in the backwoods of America it took on all the appearances of early gospel meetings, with liberal dashes of hellfire and damnation.

Language, a common language, is the key to all development. This was something that black Africans did not possess, coming from a wide tribal spectrum. The written word was non-existent and history and tradition was handed down by word of mouth. During the early part of the 18th century, English became their common tongue but as education was still denied to them, they could only express themselves clearly through music and that music came from those white people who showed them compassion and attempted to bring them hope, the Methodists. This music would eventually become known as the Negro Spiritual. The earliest 'spirituals' were simply the white hymns that spoke of salvation and eternal love, commodities in short supply to the African slave.

Throughout the 18th century the voices of those opposed to slavery grew in volume, and songs, both black and white, reflected this.

The story of The Reverend John Newton is the most incredible account of human endurance and fortitude, and in some ways mirrors the suffering of the slaves whose cause he championed in the later stages of his life. It's a long one, but perhaps when you finish it you will think it worthwhile.

Newton was born in London in July 1725. His father was a merchant sea captain who travelled the Mediterranean. From the age of eleven, young Newton made six voyages with his father until the man's retirement. In 1744, aged 19, Newton was the victim of a press gang and served on a British man o' war, HMS *Harwich*. His upbringing ensured his immediate promotion to midshipman. The conditions he found on board were intolerable. The maggot infested food and the harsh treatment of the crew were too much for him: he deserted. On recapture, his punishment was to be flogged with the cat o' nine tails before the assembled crew, and to be demoted to common seaman.

In 1746 he requested to be exchanged into service aboard a slave ship, and ended up in Sierra Leone, where he then became the servant of a slave trader. Life was even worse than before. He was physically and sexually abused and was only rescued by a sea captain who had known his father. He was soon back on a slave ship, and eventually assumed his own command. It is now important to emphasise that John Newton had no religious belief, and in view of his life thus far it was hardly surprising. He was also a serial rapist, taking any black woman he cared to. However, during one voyage home, his ship was caught in a dreadful storm and Newton experienced what he later called his 'great deliverance'. His journal states that when all seemed lost, he cried 'Lord, have mercy upon us'. Coming out of the storm he reflected on his words and believed that God had spoken to him, and that he had found 'grace'. He would never forget May 10, 1748, the day he subjected his will to a greater power, and observed it to the end of his days.

He continued to carry the 'Black Gold' across the ocean but thereafter always treated his 'cargoes' humanely. He married in 1750 and due to ill health quit the sea in 1755, taking up the post of Surveyor of Tides at Liverpool. He taught himself Latin and Greek amongst other subjects, and during his time at Liverpool met the great evangelical preacher George Whitefield, and became his fervent admirer. Through Whitefield, Newton was introduced to John Wesley, and his conversion was complete.

He decided to become a Minister himself and applied to the Archbishop of York for ordination. He was refused, but his self-education continued as he taught himself Hebrew. His persistence finally paid off when he was ordained by the Bishop of Lincoln in 1765, and was given the curacy of Olney in Buckinghamshire. His oratory and evangelical zeal was such that the church at Olney had to be enlarged to accommodate the growing congregation. The poet William Cowper came to live with him in Olney and was a great supporter of Newton's work, assisting him in services and helping to establish a series of weekly prayer meetings. At each of these meetings Newton and Cowper presented a new hymn they had written,

And what hymns! They were published as *The Olney Hymns* in 1779. *How Sweet The Name Of Jesus Sounds, Glorious Things Of Thee Are Spoken* and the one that would become an anthem not just for white congregations of Britain but also for the poor white folk of America and the Negro slave.

> *Amazing Grace (how sweet the sound)*
> *That sav'd a wretch like me*
> *I once was lost, but now am found*
> *Was blind, but now I see*

Think of Newton's life. His crimes: the flogging: the abuse: the slave trade and his subsequent conversion, and then look at these words from a different perspective.

> *Thro' many dangers, toils and snares*
> *I have already come;*
> *Tis Grace has brought me safe thus far*
> *And Grace will lead me home*

Many people today feel there is something missing in their lives. If that is so, just think what it meant to the less fortunate 200 years ago.

Amazing Grace was written around 1768 and the melody is attributed to an old Scottish air.

In 1780 John Newton took up his new position as rector of St Mary Woolnoth, in the City of London. He continued to draw and influence, large congregations, one of their number being William Wilberforce, who subsequently became the leader of the British anti-slavery movement.

Amazing Grace was taken up almost immediately as both a white and black anthem and has endured to this day. It was the closing song of the great Live Aid concert in 1985, sung by the black opera singer Jessie Norman. How ironic that a concert in aid of starving Africans should close with a song written by a white slave captain and performed by a black artist. Although blind, Newton gave evidence to the Commission for the abolition of slavery at St. James's Palace in 1805 and continued to preach up until the last year of his life, when 'grace' finally led him home in 1807, the year slavery was abolished in Britain.

At about the same time that Newton was writing his hymns, the blacks themselves were composing their own songs, or Spirituals. One of the earliest was written in tribute to another clergyman, Bishop Francis Asbury. Asbury was a member of the Methodist Episcopal Church in the Colonies, and devoted much of his time to helping and educating the slaves, who saw him as a latter day Moses. To this end they composed a Spiritual entitled *Go Down Moses* around 1790.

> *Oh take your shoes from off your feet, Let my people go*
> *And walk into the golden street, Let my people go*
> *Go down Moses, way down in Egypt land*
> *Tell ol' Pharaoh, let my people go*

As with many popular songs, this one had a 'second coming'. In the 1850s the 'underground railroad', the routes used by escaping slaves, helped by Abolitionists, was in full swing. Many of these abolitionists were Quakers, a movement started by George Fox in the 17th century. They did not observe the sacraments but believed in helping their fellow man. The Pennsylvania Quakers were doing just that and are credited with actually starting these escape routes which resulted in over 40,000 slaves reaching safety in Canada. A black woman from the North, Harriet Tubman, made legendary incursions into the South to bring out the slaves, and was nicknamed General Tubman by the zealot John Brown. *Go Down Moses* was now dedicated to her and in the coming Civil War it was taken up as an anthem by black regiments serving with the Union armies.

The original Negro Spirituals were not officially recognised until the first book of spirituals was published in 1871, the same year that the Fisk Jubilee Singers, the first black university choir, toured America and Europe. The last time I heard *Go Down Moses*, was in a little prep school in Northumberland in 1998. I had lectured there and the following morning at prayers, the choir (all white) sang it especially for me. From Bishop Asbury and General Tubman, to the Fisk Singers and Mowden Hall Preparatory School, in all spanning 200 years. That is the strength of the popular song and its effect on our culture.

It is impossible to say who first came up with the bizarre idea of a white man 'blacking up' and impersonating a Negro. Perhaps it is no more bizarre than the many races that sported war paint at some stage in their history or both women and men wearing make-up, or Regency Bucks wearing outrageous wigs. It really doesn't matter, but what does matter is why they did. Firstly the fascination between black and white was, and is ever present. If you are black you look at a black heavyweight boxer or basketball player and think him invincible set against a puny white opponent: a definite case of 'white men can't jump'. If you are white you look at a white physicist or university don and see them as infinitely more intelligent than a corresponding black academic. This is surely generalisation and racial stereotyping, but if we are honest with ourselves, we will admit that <u>both</u> races hold these 'truths' to be self-evident. It is all very sad, but it is a fact of life.

From the slave days to Civil Rights, many white prejudices were ridiculous in the extreme and from the black perspective most whites are seen as racists, and the sole perpetrators of the slave trade. Sex, fear and ignorance always fuelled racial hatred, and still do, but now an equally absurd 'positive' discrimination attempts to redress the balance and fails miserably. How many times does one read today that 'the white man stole the black man's music'? Why do we accept it without question? How can you 'steal' anything that does not 'belong' to anyone in the first place?

30

Did Marlowe or Bacon write some of Shakespeare's plays? Did W. C. Handy, the Father of The Blues, steal his songs from Memphis street singers? Does Lloyd Webber plagiarise Chopin or Mozart? Almost certainly, but we can't prove it beyond doubt, and if we could we still would not care! We cannot accept it as an absolute truth, nor should we.

The truth lies elsewhere and it is the real reason for the creation of 'nigger' minstrels. No one disputes the inherent rhythm of the Negro or the unashamed raw emotion in their songs. Why is it that a black gospel choir can make a hymn come alive and make you feel joyful, while the same hymn sung by a white choir sounds flat in comparison? What is it that the average black dancer has that makes the white equivalent look clumsy and totally uncool? Put simply it is style, a style soaked in soul. What the white man 'stole' is the black man's style. Listen to the Minstrels, listen to the great white bandleaders, and listen to Presley, Dusty Springfield, Mick Jagger and a thousand others. It is clear and unimpeachable.

The actual music is a completely different question. Why is it so hard to accept that the development of popular music crossed racial divides? Can some Blues roots be found in the lament of Celtic pipes? Did Ragtime come out of the 'honky tonk' sounds played in the saloon bars of American frontier towns? Was Jazz influenced by John Philip Sousa's military music, and possibly even German 'Oom Pah' bands? The answer to all these questions is, probably. Anything as culturally diverse as popular music will draw its influences from any source available over a great period of time. Are we any the poorer for admitting these probabilities? Of course not, unless you stick your head in the sands of time and subscribe to racial intolerance, whatever colour you happen to be. Music is and has always been, colour blind.

The disagreements between the Colonists and the Mother Country over taxes and social welfare, culminated in the American Declaration of Independence in 1776. One of the songs most clearly associated with the ensuing war is *Yankee Doodle*. So American, so jingoistic. In fact it is neither. It was written by an Englishman, a British Army surgeon Dr Richard Shuckburg, and is based on the English nursery rhyme *Lucy Locket*. The lyrics are less than flattering to the Americans, portraying them as ignorant fools. It was yet another excuse for the British to indulge their superiority complex.

Yankee Doodle came to town riding on a pony
Stuck a feather in his cap and called it macaroni.

The fight for independence has itself become a victim of the re-writing of history. Today's Hollywood influenced children see it as a battle between Americans and their overlords, the British. Actually it should be seen in terms of a civil war, since both sides were from the same stock, British. To give you some idea of just how 'British' the rebels were, you need look no further than an American Musical Primer written by Andrew Law in 1793, after independence, when he condemned American native music as 'harsh'.

The only quality in the arts, architecture and the social graces was still seen to emanate from the Mother Country. After 1776, America may have been independent but as far as their cultural base was concerned it still rested in Britain.

At home in Britain, throughout the 18th century, the popular music scene was split by class division. A royal edict had proclaimed that 'common' music should not be performed in theatres, which were reserved for drama, comedy and 'serious' music. The only places where the ordinary person could enjoy their 'folk' or pop songs were the inns and hostelries.

This marginalisation would result in the wonderful phenomenon of Music Hall in the 19th century and the great theatres, which all contained long bars as evidence of their 'licensed' antecedents. I will deal with this singularly British phenomenon in a later chapter.

Now let us return to the 'Nigger Minstrel'. As early as 1790 there is evidence of this peculiar manifestation, but it was in 1822, that English actor Charles Mathews, staged a one-man show in black face. Mathews had travelled in America, picking up ideas for new songs and dances. He attended a show at the African Theatre, New York, where he saw a performance of *Hamlet*. He was fascinated to hear the audience, triggered by Hamlet's line, 'and by opposing end them', call for a plantation song, *Opossum Up A Gum Tree,* with the words 'and by opposum, endum!' His subsequent one man show, *A Trip To America,* may have been the first appearance on stage of the 'black face minstrel'....and it happened in London!

Celtic Bard (above left); medieval troubadours; section of the Bayeux tapestry (below).

Early lute player (above, left); Geoffrey Chaucer;
Chaucer manuscript (below)

Thomas Tallis (above);
William Caxton's printing press

Henry VIII (above);
John Newton (below)

16th century slave ship arriving in North America (above)
Slave auction (below)

Thomas Rice ('Jim Crow')

Edwin Christy Minstrels poster

Stephen Foster

P.T. Barnum and dwarf

The original Black & White Minstrels

I WISH I WAS IN

DIXIE'S LAND

Written and Composed expressly for

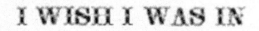

Bryant's Minstrels

BY

DAN. D. EMMETT.

Arranged for the Pianoforte by

W. L. HOBBS,

NEW-YORK:
Published by FIRTH, POND & CO., No. 547 Broadway.

Boston   Buffalo   Rochester   Cleveland
OLIVER DITSON   C. L. PUTNAM   J. P. WEBSTER   S. BRAINARD & SONS

Entered according to Act of Congress A.D. 1860.

However, perhaps the first acknowledged 'black face' performer was Thomas Dartmouth 'Daddy' Rice. He owned a theatre in Louisville, Kentucky, and while watching the antics of a black stable boy jumping around and singing in the back yard, got the idea of painting his face black and presenting what he called a 'Minstrel' show. He was on to a winner, not simply because of the white's fascination with blacks but also because blacks could not perform on a stage because they were slaves. It also comforted the whites to have their prejudices confirmed that slaves were simple, ignorant and vastly inferior. Rice's portrayal of the Negro as a cavorting 'golliwog' is evident in the lyrics of his stage character Jim Crow:

> *Wheel about an' turn about an' do jis so,*
> *An' ebery time ah wheel about ah jump Jim Crow.*
> Thomas Rice, 1826

The melody sounded like, and in fact was, an old British folk song and the London *Times* review of the show in 1832 even commented that it contained elements of 'Scotch snivel, Hibernian whoops and English guffaw'. NB: There may well have been a real Jim Crow.

Harry Reynolds writes in his 1928 book, *Minstrel Memories,* that the son of two re-captured slaves who had been burned alive as punishment for escaping, became a busker on the streets of New York in the 1770s. He played fiddle and performed his own dance, the Yambo Yam. He was so successful that he was able to retire to Virginia with his white wife and his own slaves! He called himself Jim Crow.

It is very likely that Thomas Rice took his character from this man, and I am indebted to my old friend Ian Whitcomb, musicologist extraordinaire, for recounting the above in his epic music industry book, *After The Ball.*

From 'hicksville' USA and the black-faced Minstrel we can see the beginnings of a new business, a 'show' business . Britain may have still ruled, creatively, but the times were a-changing. In 1828 John Hill Hewitt wrote the first successful American pop song, *The Minstrel's Return From The War*, and in the same year Sarah Hale wrote the first American anti-slave novel, *Northwood*. Now America was beginning to confront its own problems and in doing so it would discover its own identity.

The solitude of the Eastern mountain ranges had harboured the British folk song for 200 years but now new 'native' songs were gaining in popularity. From Kentucky came a group of melodies known as The Lonesome Tunes, one of which is the haunting blues tinged *Darlin' Cory*.

Wake up wake up darlin' Cory,
What makes you sleep so sound.
The revenue officers comin'
He's gonna tear your still house down

Wake up wake up darlin' Cory,
Stop hanging round my bed.
Bad likkers ruin'd my body,
Pretty women ruin'd my head

In retrospect you can hear the emotion and anguish of the urban blues of the 1930s in this song. The subject matter is the same... poverty, alcohol, rejection: in fact *Darlin' Cory* is about a ghost, as was the old 16th century English folk tune, *Widdecomb Fair*. Was this 'white' blues? Whatever, it <u>was</u> native American music.

In the early 1840's the solo black-faced troubadours had transformed into large groups of travelling musicians, comics and dancers. These groups were called the 'Nigger Minstrels'. Surprisingly most of them were Northeners, and they were as popular in the big cities of the North as they were in the frontier townships across the Mississippi. Perhaps their most enduring image is as entertainment on board the big river stern-wheelers. The riverboat captains used them to persuade the Ohio farm boy and the Boston clerk to give in to adventure and go west.

The first of these groups to be truly successful were The Virginia Minstrels, and one of its members, New Yorker Daniel Decatur Emmett, would go on to even greater heights. Perhaps these were the first true examples of bands on the road. Most certainly it was the first example of a true native American theatre genre. They were self- contained, playing banjos, derived from the African 'banja' or 'banjila', 'bones', tambourines, fiddles and pennywhistles. They danced, they played and they sang. They were big business. Very often their songs, evoking the romantic down home feel of the Deep South showed a basic contempt for the negro as a figure of ridicule and often as not bordered on the obscene. Fortunately this was not always the case. Some still stayed true to their Appalachian/British folk roots, singing songs like *Turkey In The Straw*.

Turkey in the hay pile, Turkey in the straw
Rake em' up and shake em' up
Anyway at all
Turkey in the hay stack Turkey in the straw.

By 1842 when John Tyler was President and the West was being opened up, the new name on everybody's lips was Edwin 'Pops' Christy. He thought that 'good ol' folk music would take on a new lease of life with group harmonies and real performance. He was right and his group, Christy's Minstrels became the longest running show to date in the annals of American theatre. *The Mousetrap*? Christy's Minstrels were still playing Broadway in 1921, 80 years after their inception !

We have Ed Christy to thank for an even more important development in popular music. In the early 1850's he helped to boost the career of a man who would become known as the Father of the Popular Song, Stephen Foster. Foster was also a Northerner, from Pittsburgh, and the only experience he had of southern life was watching the slaves work at his father's warehouse. He had been to music school but had dropped out. That didn't matter, because what Stephen Foster had was a natural song writing talent. His first songs were ballads in the British style, like his first hit published in 1844, *Open Thy Lattice Love*. But then he actually began to write about America, specifically the Southern States and a southern ideal of ante-bellum houses and loveable 'darkie' slaves. This may have been unfashionable but it was the key to his great success with minstrel opuses like *Camptown Races, Oh Susannah, Swanee River*, and *The Old Folks At Home*.

The other thing that set Foster apart from earlier folk inspired pop, was his inclusion of an obvious chorus that you could hum or whistle after a couple of hearings. Prior to this, most folk songs were 'story songs', told through a series of verses.

Through the 1850s, Christy's Minstrels made these songs hits not just in America but in Britain too, and in doing so made Foster the first great pop writer. He was also the first to be paid a royalty of 2 cents on every copy sold of sheet music embodying his compositions. This certainly beat the $15 Christy paid him for the rights to *Swanee River* in 1851. After this, Foster became disillusioned with sleepy Southern imagery and its attendant racial overtones and refused to write any more offensive dialect songs. He even refused to permit his sheet music copies to carry cartoons of blacks as figures of ridicule. His later songs like, *Nelly Was A Lady* and *Old Dog Tray*, portrayed the slaves with dignity and compassion.

He was probably also affected by the comments in Dwight's *Journal Of Music* in 1852, which read:

Foster's tunes are only skin deep, hummed and whistled without musical emotion. They persecute and hunt the morbidly sensitive nerves of musical persons so that they too hum them and whistle them involuntarily, hating them even while they hum them.

A true cynics view of the pop song.

In 1850, the great showman, Phineas T. Barnum, brought a Swedish singer over to America, and made her a star. Jennie Lind was billed as 'The Swedish Nightingale', and her performances included songs by Bellini, Rossini… and Stephen Foster.

Many writers think it is better not to read their reviews, but unfortunately Foster was not one of them. He concentrated on becoming what he perceived to be a 'quality' songwriter, and left the Minstrel world behind him. He tried and mostly failed, dying from alcohol abuse in the Bowery, New York City in 1864. Not only was Foster the Father of Pop, he was also the first 'rock star' to kill himself through one excess or other! Sadly, the last song he wrote was a perfect epitaph, *Beautiful Dreamer*.

> *Beautiful dreamer wake unto me*
> *Starlight and dewdrops are waiting for thee*
> *Sounds of the rude world heard in the day*
> *Lulled by the moonlight have all passed away. .*
> Stephen Foster

Well before the American Civil War, popular music was delineating the stark contrast between North and South.

The Hutchinson Family were a group of traditional folk singers, sister Abby and brothers Judson, Asa and John, who rather than 'black up', sang an eclectic mixture of Anglo/American folk songs, plantation tunes and even Victorian ballads. They came from New Hampshire and from 1841 to 1859 toured America and England and even performed at the White House for President Tyler. They also had something else far more potent in their musical armoury, the Protest Song. They took up the cause of Abolitionism and supported the ranting John Brown, he of 'mouldering in the grave' fame. Brown had come to Kansas in 1855 and set up the local militia to stamp out slavery on the Kansas/Missouri border.

He murdered and pillaged in the name of God and abolitionism until his execution in Charleston, Virginia for treason, murder and the slave insurrection at Harpers Ferry in 1859. His last words had a terrifying ring of truth about them:

I John Brown, am now quite certain that the crimes of this guilty land will never be purged away but with blood. I had, as I now think, vainly flattered myself that without very much bloodshed it might be done.

The Hutchinson family popularised a song written by George Root which became an anthem for the North in the coming war, and has since served Americans equally well from Iwo Jima to Sicily, *The Battle Cry Of Freedom*:

The Union forever, hurrah boys hurrah,
Down with the traitor, up with the Star
While we rally round the flag boys
We'll rally once again
Shouting the battle cry of freedom.

This song and others similar, were sung by the Hutchinsons at freedom and abolitionist rallies across the Northern States. When they took their music a little further south, riots ensued resulting in bloodshed. This, and John Brown's death at Harpers Ferry, persuaded the Hutchinsons to disband as a group in 1859.

Strangely enough, that same year brought the first airing of a song that would become the rallying cry for all the Good Ol' Boys of the South or at least it would after the Civil War. But allegedly it was never intended to be a Southern anthem, unlike *The Bonnie Blue Flag*. Daniel Decatur Emmett, he of minstrel fame and friend of Stephen Foster, wrote a song which was published in 1860 and performed by Emmett's group at the time, Bryant's Minstrels. It became so popular that both Presidents, Lincoln in the North and Jefferson Davis in the South, had it played at their respective inaugurations.

> *Oh I wish I was in de land ob cotton*
> *Old times dar am not forgotten*
> *Look away, look away, look away Dixie Land*
> *Den I wish I was in Dixie! Hooray! Hooray!*
> *In Dixie's land we'll take our stand to lib an' die in Dixie*
> *Away! Away! away down south in Dixie.*

The song's first stanza was actually rejected by the publishers on religious grounds. Read them and you can understand why.

> *Dis worl' was made in jiss six days, an' finished up in various ways*
> *Look away! Look away! Look away! Dixie Land*
> *Dey den made Dixie trim and nice, but Adam called it 'Paradise'*
> *Look away!* Etc.

I said earlier that Dixie was never intended to be a Southern rallying cry. There was a much earlier form of political correctness at work here, or was it just simple self- preservation? Apparently Daniel Emmett's father had helped to found the 'underground railway' escape system for the slaves, and Daniel himself was a self confessed supporter of emancipation long before it became fashionable... allegedly. If this was truly the case, I do not know what to make of the original lyrics, long since removed:

> *In Dixie land de darkies grow*
> *If white folks only plant dar toe*
> *Look away! etc*
> *Dey wet de groun' wid' bakker smoke*
> *Den up de darkies heads will poke*
> *Look away!* Etc.

For an abolitionist Mr Emmett certainly wrote some overtly racist lyrics. Nonetheless he was said to be 'mortified' by the adoption of his songs by the Confederacy. What is just as interesting is the origin of the word Dixie. Many thought it referred to the Pennsylvania-Maryland boundary surveyed between 1763 and 1767 to settle a land dispute involving two families, the Calverts of Maryland and the Penns of Pennsylvania. The two British surveyors, Charles Mason and Jeremiah Dixon gave their names to this line, which later designated the divide between the slave and the free States, the Mason-Dixon Line.

Alternatively there are those who say that the ten dollar bill produced by The Citizen's Bank and Trust Company of Louisiana, had the French word 'dix' printed on the back of the bill, and that from then on Louisiana, a former French colony, was referred to as 'dix's' land.

The other alternative is far more in keeping with this book. In Derbyshire, England, there is a house called Normanton House that used to belong to a wealthy family called Dix. They paid for many poor souls to emigrate to America in the early 19th century. Then, one of the Dix's emigrated to the Northern States. He then moved down South taking his workers with him, and became a rich plantation owner. Picking cotton was not to their liking and they used to chant 'Want to go back to old Dix's land! This is borne out by relatives of Emmett who lived 'next door' to a family called the Snowdens. All six Snowden children were musicians and on the grave stones of two of them, Ben and Lew, it is said an inscription read: 'They taught Dixie to Dan Emmett'.

You can take your pick as to which story you want to believe. For me, I'll go for a combination of the last two. It has all the veracity of a real folk tradition. A song is handed down from generation to generation, until it metamorphosed into legend. Wherever it came from, Dan Emmett is credited with being the first person ever to use the word Dixie publicly. Elvis Presley sang it in American Trilogy in the 1970s and for some inexplicable reason English 'good ol' boys' from Cornwall to Yorkshire are still riding around with Dixie stickers fixed to their rear bumpers, and/or the Confederate flag flying from their car aerials. Oh well, once a hit always a hit.

The story behind another song whose origins have become obscured through the years, is well worth telling. The word 'chariot' is French and means a sled or truck for transporting goods. A 'chariot' is what the slaves used to pull tobacco out of the fields and they came to believe a large 'chariot' would one day swing them away to heaven. In 1847 a young slave called Sarah Sheppard was sitting on the banks of the Wabash River in Tennessee with her three-year-old daughter, contemplating suicide. They were going to be parted by their owner and Sarah could not face the agony. Apparently an old 'black' mama saw them, and realising what was about to happen, rushed over and said "Don't you do it honey. One day the Chariot of the Lord is gonna swing low. There's great work for this baby to do here on earth. She's gonna stand before Kings and Queens. Don't you do it honey". She didn't 'do' it and they were both separated.

Twenty-five years later, her baby Ella, became the pianist for the Jubilee Singers, the choir of the first black University, Fisk in Nashville. They were the first black group of any kind to appear at a huge musical festival, The World Peace Jubilee, held in Boston in 1867. They also appeared in Europe before Queen Victoria and the Kaiser. In the meantime her mother, who had never forgotten the words of the old black 'mama', had written *Swing Low Sweet Chariot.*

> *I looked over Jordan what did I see*
> *Comin' for to carry me home*
> *A band of angels comin' after me*
> *Comin'for to carry me home*

The happy ending to the tale is that Ella finally found her mother and they lived happily together until Sarah's death, glorying in a prophecy that was fulfilled. Every time the chorus of England fans roars out *Swing Low* at Twickenham during a rugby international, they can have no idea that the song is about winning the struggle for life which in Sarah and Ella Sheppard's case was certainly no game.

Slavery may have appeared to be the only reason for two sides to go to war but the Union was the key. The South saw themselves as a different people, rural farming stock of mainly British extraction, and gentlemen to boot, which of course was not completely untrue. The poor white trash of the South had much in common with the negro slaves. They were looked down on by the rich and harboured an unfair resentment of blacks.

This of course was a futile attempt to 'upgrade' themselves in the social strata. You always have to look down on someone, and you didn't get much lower than a negro slave. Conversely the North was the industrial engine for the continent and the home of immigrants who were beginning to pour in from across the world. One needed the other, and that 'one' would fight to keep it together. Abolitionism was the catalyst that maintained the Union. The battles would be bloody and the aftermath so painful that it would resonate to the present day, not least through music: 'redneck' and 'honky tonk' country music, the white 'trailer trash' re-action to Yankee sophistication.

Black dissatisfaction is ever present in the aggressive street lingo of Rap, Hip Hop, and the dance culture. It's a long way from John Rolfe's commentary on the first '20 negars' to arrive in North America in 1619 to the days of Civil Rights and *We Shall Overcome*. Those who came 'out of Africa' were as responsible, no more no less, as the white settlers, for the growth and beautiful diversity of popular music in that first 250 years. It would be people escaping thousands of years of slavery who would shape it over the next one hundred and fifty.

4

The Old Folk Back Home

In the previous chapter I concentrated on America, devoting little to the 'home front'. If this gave the impression that nothing of note on the music front was occurring in Britain during the period, please read on.

An Italian art form arrived via France early in the 18th century. Originally called the Commedia dell Arte, it was essentially a performance of comedy sketches, with the added attraction of song and dance. Apart from such traditional characters as Harlequin and Columbine, mentioned many times by Shakespeare, this new theatre form showcased a host of others like Pantaloon and a servant Pulchinello. The latter would become the first clown, and also give his name to a great British institution, Punch and Judy. Pantaloon would also give his name to the most enduring form of British theatre still popular today.

Because language was a problem in the early days of the Commedia dell Arte, the British performances relied on mime, and also included more music and dance. This hybrid musical theatre became known as Pantomime.

In 1717, the first pantomime, a ballet, called *The Loves of Mars and Venus*, was presented at the Lincoln's Inn Fields Theatre. But it was the great David Garrick who, in 1773, gave us the first real pantomime, *Jack and The Giant Killer*, at the Theatre Royal, Drury Lane. However, the true 'king' of Pantomime was undoubtedly the great Italian, Joseph Grimaldi. Appearing in London for the first time in 1800, he captured the hearts of theatregoers with his catchy songs, and comedy routines. He is also said to have pioneered the phenomenon of cross-dressing, bringing the first pantomime Dame to the stage. Shakespeare would have had something to say on that subject. His female characters were always portrayed by men. Joseph Grimaldi also has one other claim to fame. The first clowns were called 'joeys', a diminutive of Joseph.

In the early part of the 18th century, popular music in Britain was rigorously controlled. A royal edict had proclaimed only the more serious forms of music were worthy of 'live' performance in the theatres of the day. To combat this unfairness, music of the people was performed for the people outdoors! For nearly a century, open air concerts were the rage, with the 'shows' at the Vauxhall Pleasure Gardens in London regularly attracting thousands. The music played was a mixture of folk, bawdy tavern songs and ballads, and the programme included jugglers, mime artistes and any speciality act that fitted the bill, literally.

But by 1859, the Vauxhall Gardens had closed, and popular music was about to move indoors. Charles Morton, a London publican, had a brainwave; he would convert his pub in Lambeth, into a place of music; a music hall. In 1861, Morton opened his first purpose built venue in London, the Oxford Music Hall. He utilised the trappings of the saloon bar to get around antiquated laws, the result being that all British music halls boasted a long bar either down one side of the theatre or across the back of the stalls. By 1868 there were over 200 music theatres/pubs in London alone, and Charles Morton rightly became known as the 'father of the halls'.

From then on, the differences between American and British popular music can be seen clearly. In the States, folk and other ethnic music became part of the mainstream, whilst in Britain we all but forgot our folk heritage as the industrial revolution brought more and more people to the cities. America was a new, thrusting society, eager to promote its own culture, whereas the 'old' country was exactly the opposite; a land of conservatism, a solid Victorian institution.

Earlier in the 18th century, a financial disaster was the catalyst for another interesting musical development. Actually it was the first financial disaster to affect the common man in a new, thrusting capitalist society, the South Sea Bubble.

The South Sea Company was formed in 1711 by the Tories, as an alternative to the Whig controlled Bank of England. The idea was that investors should profit from the new and lucrative trading in the South Seas. It was a great idea, lent credibility by the Anglo-Spanish Treaty of 1713, which gave the new company a monopoly of the Spanish slave trade and access to the rich Spanish American markets. It was a classic case of the get rich quick scheme, where those in first could unload at a vast profit as the shares rose. The only way this could work was by attracting thousand of new, often small, investors. The shares went through the roof, and collapsed spectacularly in 1720, leaving thousands in penury.

But what does all this have to do with music? In 1728, John Gay presented his 'opera', *The Beggars Opera*, in London. It was an allegory of the time, but its real theme was the capitalist disaster of the South Sea Bubble. It was rumoured that the main character, MacHeath, was based on Tory Prime Minister Robert Walpole, who presided over the sorry financial fiasco. Whether this was Gay's intention is of no matter: the British public saw it that way.

It clearly depicted the court of George II as a kind of thieves kitchen; the morality of the ruling class was put on a par with that of London's underworld.
The Oxford Illustrated History Of Britain

So here was the first example of 1980s and 90s Tory sleaze, and the Wall Street ethic of 'show me the money' culture. *The Beggars Opera* was a satirical indictment of a system out of control, and would continue to inspire others of like mind right through to the Weimar Republic in the 1920's, with Kurt Weill and Berthold Brecht's reworking of the piece as *The Threepenny Opera*. I wonder if Louis Armstrong, Bobby Darin and many others had any idea what they were singing when they recorded *Mac The Knife*. I doubt it, but they did makes loads of money.

To summarize; the differences between British and American popular music in the 19th century centred on the peculiar denial in Britain of our musical roots. Folk music was all but forgotten as rural life gave way to the Industrial Revolution and urbanisation. Music Hall became the 'new' folk, with a dash of city sophistication that surprisingly crossed all class barriers.

In America, ethnic and rural music made their way into the mainstream of theatre and showbusiness, via the minstrel shows and a subsequent American version of music hall, Vaudeville. Throughout the 18th century, America had believed that British and European artistic influences were the only ones of any import. Now, at last, America was at ease with its own 'culture'; a multi-ethnic pop culture.

By 1864, Stephen Foster, the 'Father of the Popular Song' was dead and British theatre was roaring ahead with Music Hall and Pantomime. But it was locked into a time warp: a cosy fireside British time warp. It would take the influence of another group of immigrants in America to shake things up.

5

Rags To Riches

Music in America during the 19th century was a fascinating contradiction. It had all the elements of the established British and other European folk forms, plus the more aesthetic and artistic sounds of hymns, and Victorian parlour songs. This was commercially viable music, personified by Stephen Foster, but alongside it sat an amazing variety of seemingly uncommercial and untaught musical styles.

Poor whites and black slaves were whooping and hollering at revival meetings, clapping hands and using instruments like the fiddle, guitar and anything percussive, in extraordinary and unconventional ways. Banjos were plucked viciously: guitars were hit as they were strummed: tambourines were jangled and feet stomped. By any other name this was rock and roll, jazz, the blues, and any other form of 20th century pop. This is why the origins of popular music development are so hard to pin down. We simply cannot say where some genre or other actually began.

Cecil Sharpe, the British folk archivist, 'found' hordes of our native folk songs alive and well in Kentucky in the 1920s. To be more specific, one county in particular held more than any other, Harlan County. Between 1825 and 1830, a group of songs written by white men, encompassed elements of folk, country and blues. Collectively they were known as the Lonesome Tunes, and later became known as the White Blues of Kentucky. The lyrics are certainly blues tinged, and the keening vocals are present today in the Bluegrass music of Kentucky.

Out 'West', cowboys took old melodies and re-wrote their own versions, in their own image.

> *As I walked out on the streets of Laredo,*
> *As I walked out in Laredo one day.*
> *I saw a young cowboy all dressed in white linen,*
> *All dressed in white linen, and cold as the clay.*

The Streets of Laredo was undoubtedly a cowboy song....or was it? Its writer did not bother to change the chorus:

> *Beat the drum slowly,*
> *And play the fife lowly*

There were no 'drums and fifes' in the old West. The origins of the song are British/Irish. It was a 17th century British military funeral song, called *The Unfortunate Rake*.

In the vast American hinterland, bar room pianists were playing up tempo music alongside the old ballads. Black writer James Bland, wrote *Oh Dem Golden Slippers* in 1857, and it was and is, Ragtime bordering on Honky Tonk, long before either style was given a name. Put in a 'class' context, the crude, uneducated music of the people, was a million years away from the sedate, sexless and proper songs of the middle and upper classes. Seen in a 'race' context, it is surely obvious that this eclectic mix of emotion and music was evenly spread between black and white.

Three things were about to bring this 'back road' music into the mainstream. Technology was the first.

In 1877, Thomas Edison patented his phonograph. He had 'discovered' how to record sound two years earlier, in his quest to invent the telephone. Within ten years, German/American, Emile Berliner had moved on from Edison's roll of wax, and invented the 'flat disc', the record. An industry was born.

As I have mentioned earlier, Music Hall reigned supreme in Britain through the 19th century, but in America, its equivalent took a little longer to arrive.

Vaudeville took its name from the 15th century French satirical song style termed *Chanson du vau de vire*, which in modern parlance means 'songs that go with the flow'. This was quickly, and judiciously corrupted to 'vau de ville'. Americans, being American, quickly ran these words together....to sound more American. Tony Pastor, opened his first 'Opera House' in The Bowery in New York in 1865. He preferred the name 'variety' rather than Vaudeville, since his approach was to introduce newcomers amongst the established stars. By 1887, New York was full of variety theatres, and they were spreading across America. Just as in Britain, pubs, known as 'free and easies', converted to variety halls, and these venues pioneered a new venture, round the clock, all day programming. The two men responsible for this questionable development were Benjamin Keith and the infamous Edward Albee. Albee became the most hated man in showbusiness because he stole, connived and pirated other people's work.

At the same time, millions more immigrants were coming to America, looking for freedom, safety and riches. They came from all over, but one group in particular would influence the course of popular music more than any other: the Eastern European Jew. Those of you familiar with the musical *Fiddler On The Roof*, will understand. Jews were being massacred in their Russian homeland, and those lucky enough to escape the 'pogroms', as they were known, landed at Ellis Island, New York in their thousands in the 1880s. Some of them were musicians, and some astute businessmen, versed in the ways of European business. They observed the rich American music scene, embraced it and its language, and added a dash of their own musical culture, the melancholy and beautiful sounds of their mother country. They were set to commercialise the melting pot of native American music.

One such man was Harry von Tilzer. Tilzer was both songwriter and businessman, and together with other of like mind, founded the home of pop music, in a street by the railroad flats in New York. 28th Street quickly became known as Tin Pan Alley, a name thought up, allegedly, by Monroe Rosenfeld, a journalist, who, noting the cacophony of sound in the street as a different song was 'plugged' to a prospective buyer, thought the result on a hot summers day, was like the sound of tin cans being banged together. There is an alternative explanation that goes back much further, to Georgian times in England, when the first real publishing trade of 'broadside ballads' got under way, and the popular music of the day was likened to cheap tin pans. Take your choice.

Tilzer wrote over 3,000 songs, and used the Alley's proximity to Broadway to sell his and others songs to the stars of the day. Other Jewish businessmen, who had been making a living selling anything in demand, from clothing to household appliances, saw the potential of pop and crossed over. An industry was born.

The first million selling song, in sheet music terms of course, was as number written by Chas K. Harris, *After The Ball*. This great old number retained the dignity of the Victorian ballad and the waltz. It was touching and polite, and co-incidentally became a hit in the very year Coca Cola was designated a soft drink rather than a 'snake remedy'.

This was still music in 'the old style', but some of the new Jewish immigrants would help music take a different direction, and would also turn out to be the greatest pop songwriters of all time. One such was Israel Baline, a Russian, brought to the new country by his parents in 1892. He would change his name, when old enough, to sound more American, even though Irving Berlin sounded vaguely German. Another arrival, a few years later, was tiny Jacov Gershvon from the Ukraine, later to become known as George Gershwin. How wonderful to think that America owed much of it's 20th century musical dominance to a Russian and a Ukranian!

The catalyst that finally brought together the American 'native' music styles, the British/European traditional songs, and the commercial acumen of the Jewish immigrants, was a syncopated dance craze, Ragtime. Simply meaning a 'ragged' or broken up beat, Ragtime was to shape the future of pop.

> Got more troubles than I can stand,
> Ever since ragtime truck the land,
> Never saw the like in all my days
> Everybody's go the ragtime craze
> > Jefferson & Roberts, 1899

In no time at all, the critics, representing clean white America, were up in arms:

A wave of vulgar, filthy and suggestive music has inundated the land. The pabulum of theatre and summer hotel orchestras is 'coon' music. Nothing but ragtime prevails and the Cakewalk, with its obscene posturings, its lewd gestures. It is artistically and morally depressing and should be suppressed by press and pulpit.

Musical Courier, 1899

This was the old Puritanism rearing its ugly racist and class head well above the parapet. Middle America was as strictly divided along social lines, as the Europeans, and the sight of the young doing the cakewalk and turkeytrot, the dances associated with Ragtime, incensed them. It was un-American for God's sake!

The ridiculous thing was, Ragtime was the first truly American music to dominate the Western World. What the Puritans hated was where it came from, the brothels and honky tonk joints, and the people who played, wrote and performed it: the supposed 'musical illiterates'. And who were these 'illiterates?' Naturally the poor black and white Americans who were playing piano in a bewildering style. Not just content with 'ragging' the beat, these guys played so fast, their left hand especially was a blur. The new sound emerged first in Southern cities like New Orleans and Memphis, the Mississippi Delta, the real melting pot. These guys had no real musical knowledge, just an incredible 'feel', and what they lacked in expertise they more than made up for with enthusiasm and energy. They were no more no less than innovators. The second group of 'illiterates' were supposedly the Jews.

Is this racist? Of course it is, but racism is as old as time, and the extraordinary thing about humans is that we practice it regardless of the lessons of history, and regardless of whichever race we belong to!

It was Irving Berlin who said: "The syncopated, shoulder shaking type of vocal and instrumental melody, which has now been dignified internationally as 'typical American music' is not wholly, or even largely, of African origin as is popularly supposed. Our popular songwriters and composers are not negroes. Many of them are of Russian birth and ancestry. All of them are of pure white blood." And this from a member of the much maligned Jewish race, in 1920! Perhaps he tried to make amends, realising what he had actually said, when he continued as follows:

50

"As in the case of everything else American, their universally popular music is the product of a sort of musical melting pot. Their distinctive school is a combination of the influences of Southern plantation songs, of European music from almost countless countries and of the syncopation that is found in the music of innumerable nationalities. Therefore, those who label our popular dance and song music as 'typical' American music hit the bulls eye in so naming it. For it is the syncopation of several lands and centuries 'Americanized'."

Berlin and Tin Pan Alley were equally on the receiving end of the racial cant they espoused:

The Jew and the Yankee stand in human temperament at polar points. Syncopated music is un- American.
Daniel Mason, music critic.

The crazy thing is, ragtime itself became polarised through just the same lofty ideals the supposed serious music critics gave voice to. A musically educated young black, Scott Joplin, born in Texas, came to prominence in 1899 with *Maple Leaf Rag*. He aspired to heights beyond the rough bar room style of ragtime, and eschewed the bar rooms and vaudeville circuit. His variety of ragtime has since become known as 'classical', and somehow, Joplin knew this would not lead to immediate success:

When I'm dead twenty five years, people are going to recognize me.
Scott Joplin

Actually, it took a lot longer. Most people, excluding pianists, only became aware of Joplin when his music was used as the backdrop to the Paul Newman movie, *The Sting*, in the 1970s.

Aside from Joplin's classical approach to ragtime, its biggest drawback was obvious: you couldn't dance to it and there were no words! Tin Pan Alley answered the call with its own hybrid form of ragtime. Taken from the real funky low down 'coon songs', which were overtly sexy, the Alley writers came up with a pop music form that set America, and Europe, dancing. Loosely termed 'bar room' ragtime, songs like *Bill Bailey Won't You Please Come Home* and Irving Berlin's first great hit, *Alexander's Ragtime Band*, set the Alley on fire. It was 1899, and the great American music machine was set to roll.

51

How different things were in Britain. Music Hall was king, and when the old Colonel 'Blimps' returned from India, Afghanistan, and Africa (you name it, we were there), they spent an evening at Morton's Oxford Theatre, or the Holborn Empire, and shed a quiet tear as Vesta Victoria sang *Waiting At The Church*. There was, however, a small similarity. But whereas our American 'cousins' had utilised the basic country sounds of their homeland to forge a new and exciting pop music, two Englishmen, who were naturally of conservative bent, decided to take serious music, in their case opera, and make it... well, slightly less serious.

Taking a genre pioneered by John Gay in the 18th century, Sir Arthur Seymour Sullivan and Sir William Schwenk Gilbert, collaborated on a series of comic operas. Gilbert, the librettist (a serious name for the lyricist), was introduced to Sullivan by the great impresario Richard D'Oyly Carte. What followed was a hugely successful run of light operas like *HMS Pinefore,* (a dig at the Admiralty), *The Mikado*, and *Pirates Of Penzance*. Sullivan, however, being English, thought he was prostituting his talents. No less a personage than Queen Victoria told him he was wasting his time! The British are famous today for 'bashing' success. Its amazing to discover we were 'at it' even then. What Victoria could not know, was that this very English partnership of Gilbert & Sullivan, would help to set the pattern of the Broadway musical, and writers like Rodgers and Hart in the 20th century. What Gilbert & Sullivan would never know was that some of their prodigious musical output would be 'stolen' by Edward Albee, the crooked impresario. Albee's dishonesty was so successful, he was able to fund many new theatres from the proceeds. In the 1890's, G & S personified British music and stage musicals, but as the new century dawned, America was leading the way.

6

Ragtime Cowboy Joe

1902, and the first million selling record of all time. It was an opera piece, *Vesti la Giubba*, sung by the greatest of all tenors, Enrico Caruso. The next resurgence of opera, in record terms, came in the 1980's with the Three Tenors, and that took a World Football Cup to take them up the charts.

Ragtime was on the rise, and the 'coon' song became a vibrant part of the genre. The master of the 'coon' style, was Ben Harney, a 'slightly' black singer/songwriter, who said he'd actually invented ragtime, but we know better. What he did was popularise the 'coon shouter' singing style that was taken up by blacks and whites alike. Here was the image of the racy, dangerous black man, with songs containing bawdy lyrics and real street slang, with titles like *If You Ain't Got No Money, Well You Needn't Com' Roun'* and *Don't Roll Those Bloodshot Eyes At Me*. This was the voice of 20th century America, but more than that, it was the birth of the pop industry.

The success of Ragtime in tandem with a record business and Tin Pan Alley, meant that market forces would now dictate a constant updating and variation of popular music to satisfy increasing demand, and that would really begin to 'muddy' the water. You could argue it had always been that way, as folk 'crossed over' with hymns and slave songs. You could also argue there had always been a commercial aspect to music with the sale of 'broadsongs' in the 16th century and the minstrel groups in the 19th, but this was something different. It was the mass marketing of music to a potentially worldwide audience.

You see, in the first half of the 19th century, popular music was quite clearly delineated. Everything, and I mean everything, up to the advent of Minstrelsy, seemed to have its origins in Britain and Ireland. But from the 1850s on, the melting pot of freed blacks, Jewish immigrants, and a music industry, created a uniquely American, as opposed to British, musical 'hotch potch'. But the language remained the same, or rather it didn't, it grew exponentially. And here's a thought: perhaps the music has never changed, only the style.

If all this seems confusing, I apologise… but believe me, you ain't read nothing yet!

The heyday of Ragtime was from 1899 to 1917, but within that same time span, two other genres of pop appeared.

The Blues, or to be specific, Country Blues, came out of the Mississippi Delta around 1911. Its 'originator' was a black Doctor of Music, W. C. Handy, from Memphis, Tennessee. However, his own band members said the good doctor was prone to walking the streets of Memphis, listening to beggars and itinerant musicians, playing their stuff on battered guitars with strange tunings, and running knife blades up and down the fretboards. Being an educated fellow, it is said he eagerly copied those down he fancied, took them away, and from that moment on claimed the copyrights!

His best known piece is said to be just such a song. Regardless, *St. Louis Blues* is probably the all time classic blues number, for which Handy will always be remembered. Actually, the song of 'his' I love the most, is known as one of the grandfathers of the Blues, *Oh Careless Love*. Now this was a steal. It started out life as a folk number, probably British, in the 18th century. By the 19th it had become a black Ohio riverboat song, and by 1914, well… Handy says he wrote it. You must judge for yourselves.

Handy's first song was written to help the election campaign of a would be Governor of Tennessee, Edward 'Boss' Crump, and was titled *Mr. Crump*. The song wasn't bad, but it certainly didn't help Crump. He lost the election, but he sure found the blues. The Blues mainly consists of the in-between notes, not quite flats, not quite sharps, in other words, a sliding scale. Three instruments lend themselves to this music style perfectly: the guitar, the fiddle, and the Celtic pipes. When a BB King or Eric Clapton bend the strings, the listener experiences a thrill we call blues or soul. They tear the very guts out of a melody. But if you also listen to the Celtic pipes, they achieve the same result, and they go back 1500 years! Even W C Handy could not have claimed any part in that!

Now, even earlier than Handy, a band emerged in Storeyville, New Orleans, playing yet another hybrid music form. Around 1905, The Original Dixieland Jazz Band was formed. They were referred to at the time, as a 'country brass band'. Surprisingly, they were white, led by trumpeter Nick La Rocca. They were one of the first true pioneers of Jazz, and formed the classic Dixieland line up of trumpet, clarinet and trombone.

By 1912 they had moved to New York, and thence to Chicago, recording the first great jazz classics, *Tiger Rag* and *Livery Stable Blues* (a million seller). Now, where did that name come from?

To many, the word jazz means sex. This is principally because black musicians, like Jelly Roll Morton and Buddy Bolden, earned their living playing in the brothels of New Orleans, hence expressions like 'I'm gonna 'jazz' you up'. However, since every music style connected with blacks from Ragtime to Rock n' Roll, is said to be a euphemism for copulation, I am going for an alternative, far more entertaining proposition.

In the deep south of the USA, the word 'just', is often pronounced 'jass'. From *Uncle Tom's Cabin* to *Gone With The Wind*, and John Grisham books, we see characters say 'Hey boy, why you doin' that?' and the answer comes, 'Jass, jass because'. It is a corruption. Thus the theory goes that when a musician was playing a certain style of rag or blues notes, someone said, 'Why you playin' that way?' and the answer came, ' Jass because'. Perhaps some journalist or music lover heard it the wrong way, and thought, hey, jazz! The hypothesis is that jazz is a corruption of a corruption!

Back to the music. Jelly Roll Morton said he had 'discovered' jazz, but then he also said he 'discovered' the blues. Handy, not to be left out, also said he 'discovered' jazz. One thing's for sure: they all owed a huge debt to the Original Dixieland Jazz Band. The great Bix Beiderbecke followed Nick La Rocca around like a star-struck fan.

What does it all mean? It means everyone was looking for new hooks to hang their musical hats on. Think about it; ragtime, blues, jazz, all emerging… at roughly the same time, and all drawing their influences from the marching music of Sousa, the street musician, the brass bands, and the 'down home' country pickers.

Put simply, it was and still is, a straightforward commercial ploy. Think today. We have Acid House, Acid Funk, Garage, Drum n' Bass, Club mix, Rap, Alt. Country, New Metal, Grunge, Hip Hop, R&B, Thrash Metal, the list goes on forever, and doesn't include all the styles around prior to 1980. And what does it all mean? Only that it is nearly all pop, recycled in one form or other, and re-titled endlessly in an attempt to give it greater significance.

Leaving commercial cynicism out of this for a moment, we must take into account the people who make it all possible, the musicians. Musicians by their very nature, love to experiment and improve themselves. Herein also lies part of the reason for changes in style. The jazz of Thelonius Monk, is light years away from Dixie, as is the progressive, if pretentious heavy rock of the 1970's from Rockabilly. Perhaps that is when music ceases to be pop, and takes itself too seriously. For the vast majority of music fans, that is not an oxymoron!

The world was now at war, and ragtime was king in America and Europe. This did not sit well with certain patriotic members of British society:

This imported heathendom!
One does not feel very national when one is hummed at, nasally, by
an alien!

Rudyard Kipling

He pulled no punches, but it was an 'age' thing. Rupert Brooke loved going to the Music Hall and listening to ragtime, in common with many of his contemporaries. What Kipling was worried about, was inevitable. Having been in thrall to British cultural development for so long, America was now in the driving seat. When they joined the Great War in 1917, they were exhorted to do so by the King of Broadway, George M. Cohan, as he sang his own song, *Over There*. How brash, how cocky, how American. Over here, we were closer to the action. We knew the full horror of the trenches. Our songs were far more poignant: *Pack Up Your Troubles, There's A Long Road Winding,* and that gentlest of patriotic rejoinders to *Keep The Home Fires Burning,* a soundtrack for doomed youth.

The writer of the last named song, was Ivor Novello. A Welshman, with matinee idol looks, Novello became the darling of the age. He was a prolific writer, and the first great British pop writer of the 20th century.

Unfortunately, in an atmosphere redolent of earlier Victorian days, his homosexuality was revealed, and after the war his career slowly went down hill. The greatest awards ceremony for songwriters in the UK today, is called the Ivors, in recognition of his musical talent, rather than his private life.

As peace came to Europe, Novello was attempting to retain his and our Britishness, through his songs, but he was fighting a losing battle. Jazz had arrived in Europe in 1917, when James Reese Europe and his Hellfighters, all servicemen, played in Paris. Shortly after, in 1919, the great ODJB toured Britain. They were a 'support' act for the great British music hall star, George Roby, the self styled 'chocolate coloured coon', in a revue called *Joy Bells* at the London Hippodrome. They blew him away, were peremptorily dismissed, and continued their tour alone, with great success.

Ragtime and now Jazz were sweeping the developed world, and the death knell of music hall and variety could be heard in the echoes of America's thrusting, vibrant music.

The process speeded up, courtesy of a British technological invention. Well, not quite wholly British. Guilielmo Marconi, an Italian living and working in Bedford, had developed 'wireless transmission' in 1895. It was intended for communication purposes, previously only possible via the telegraph.

America realised the commercial potential of this new medium, and broadcast the first music from New York around 1919.

The British Broadcasting Corporation was operating a year or so later, but by 1922 there were over 600 stations in the USA! By 1967, there were only three in the UK. At least the New World understood the value of mass marketing.

So, as we enter the Golden Age of Jazz, and the road to Rock, dwell on the conflicting statements of two 'greats' of the American music machine; Paul Whiteman, a wonderful name for the man who sanitized jazz for straight, white middle class audiences, and one of the greatest songwriters of all time, George Gershwin, Jewish immigrant

Jazz arrived in chains in America 300 years ago.
Paul Whiteman, 1922

Jazz is a product of the energy stored up in America.
George Gershwin, 1926

I leave it to the reader to make up his or her own mind as to which of these statements is politically correct, and which has the ring of truth about it.

7

Now You Has Jazz

The term 'Jazz Age', was coined by writer F. Scott Fitzgerald, and it marked the first time in popular music history that a younger generation began to make its presence felt commercially as well as culturally. 'Younger' in this instance refers generally to those in their mid-20s to 30s.

The most famous jazz musician of all time was undoubtedly Louis Armstrong. No, not because he was the best musician; there would be a million arguments about that. Louis was simply the 'face' of jazz, the man whose personality and style endeared him to countless generations.

Life didn't start out so well for Louis. In 1912 he was institutionalised for a minor misdemeanour aged 11. In the delightfully named Coloured Waif's Home, he learned to play cornet and bugle, and played in the home's brass band. It was not jazz, but he always swore those days gave him his distinctive style later on. He joined Kid Ory's band in 1919, re-placing King Oliver, whom he joined in 1922. He went on to play with Sidney Bechet, Fletcher Henderson and even a young white blues yodeller, Jimmie Rodgers, before forming his own Hot Five outfit. At that point he was a legend in the making.

Doin' my days work, pleasing the public and enjoying my horn.
Louis Armstrong

Was he the best cornet/trumpet player? No, but he was the man who drove jazz and reached a huge audience, because of his equally huge personality. Rock needed Elvis just as British pop needed the Beatles: it's all marketing.

The man who made jazz 'acceptable' to middle class America, was bandleader Paul Whiteman. Ian Whitcomb's description of Whiteman's endeavours sums it up perfectly:

Here the 'slut jazz woman' was made into a lady. She was Eliza Doolittle and Whiteman was Professor Higgins.
Ian Whitcomb, After The Ball.

Paul Whiteman had an orchestra, not a band. That shows you how 'serious' he was. His concert at New York's Aeolian Hall in 1925 attempted to marry jazz with operetta and classical styles.

The object is to show that tremendous strides have been made in popular music from the early discordant jazz to the melodious music of today. Eventually our music will become a stepping stone which will be helpful in giving the coming generations a much deeper appreciation of better music.
Paul Whiteman, 1925

This was an attempt at musical education, which showed Whiteman's misunderstanding of commercial forces. It was laudable, but misplaced. Once the public have heard the real thing, no amount of 'education' will sway them the other way.

The high spot of the Aeolian concert was the debut of *Rhapsody In Blue*, played by its composer, George Gershwin. It wasn't real jazz, but perhaps it was real pop. This ersatz white concert jazz made many aware of the 'real McCoy', black jazz. What had started out as a white/black music form with the ODJB, had become an exciting, earthy dance music. What made it even more exciting was the 18th Amendment of 1920, banning alcohol in the United States. Prohibition, and the resultant explosion of illegal drinking clubs, the speak easies, where you could hear the hottest jazz around, gave the music a dangerous, 'illegal' edge.

Meanwhile, down in the boondocks another music style was emerging in the 1920s, which also seemed to be more concerned with a more traditional, serious approach. George Dewey Hay, a journalist who had moved over into radio, started a series of Barn Dance shows for various stations, culminating in his WSM Nashville show which took its name from his opening announcement, following an opera programme:

You've just been listening to the old opry', now listen to the Grand Ol' Opry.

Dewey Hay, 1927

Country folk, mainly in the South and West of America, still hung on to their cherished British roots. They had not been exposed to the large-scale immigration in the North, and seemed to be in a time warp. Or were they? The Civil War had settled the slavery question, but this had not percolated through to many Southerners. The call of 'The South will rise again' echoed from Louisiana to Arizona, and they meant it. The South would rise again but strictly in a musical sense. The musical melting pot of black and white sounds was centred on the Southern heartland, the Mississippi Delta. Jazz, ragtime and blues may have had their origins in rural areas, but they all developed in the cities, like New Orleans and Memphis in the South, and the big Northern cities. However, in rural America, especially in the South, there was still strict segregation... not least in musical terms.

Hay allowed only 'string bands' on his Nashville show, no horns, and definitely no drums. The very first of these 'culturally acceptable' bands was the gloriously named Dr. Humphrey Bate and his Possum Hunters, with the good doctor's daughter, Alcyone, aged 13, on piano. She would remain a fixture at the Opry' for the next 50 years!

The music they played varied from ragtime to John Philip Sousa marches and religious songs, but also included many strange haunting memories from another century, and another country.

In some ways, Dewey Hay was similar to Paul Whiteman, except he was not trying to 'educate'. As he saw it, he was trying to preserve his native music, and keep it pure. As British folk archivist Cecil Sharpe discovered, our music was alive and well in Nashville in the 1920s.

Oh Brother where art thou?

Since the middle of the 19th century, country folk, black and white, had been attending outdoor prayer meetings. The blacks sang spirituals, and the whites a strange Methodist 'call and response'. Sometimes the two styles 'crossed over', with hymns like *Just A Closer Walk With Thee*, and *The Old Rugged Cross*, and they were always based on a white hymnody. In the late 19th century, the black Pentecostal Church encouraged musical accompaniment, with a strong rhythm bias, encouraging the congregations to join in.

By the 1920s this black church music had become a style called Gospel. A Baptist minister's son, Thomas A. Dorsey coined the name Gospel Songs. One of his great innovations was to accompany hymns outside the churches, with hired singers literally helping to sell his songs. And what songs they were. With over 1,000 to his credit, the most notable are *Peace In The Valley*, and *Take My Hand Precious Lord*. I was recently singing along in a black Pentecostal church on a tiny Bahamian island. It was a tribute to Dorsey, right down to the rhythm section and the glorious singing. If only all religion were like this.

Don't put your daughter on the stage Mrs Worthington!

Broadway was a long way from the gospel sounds of the South, and not just in miles. The stage musical had found its inspiration in Edwardian England, when impresario George Edwards presented his musicals, *Gaiety Girls* and *The Arcadians*, still irrepressibly British. The theatre district in New York had become centred on Broadway and 40th Street, since the opening of the Empire Theatre by Charles Frohman in 1893. The term 'The Great White Way', was coined by advertising guru O. J. Gude in 1901, and referred to the glowing white lights illuminating the thoroughfare.

The Tin Pan Alley writers found a natural, and lucrative home on Broadway, and of course it had far greater artistic integrity than its more basic, earthy predecessor, Vaudeville. Irving Berlin wrote his first Broadway score in 1914, called *Watch Your Step*, and George Gershwin made his debut there with *La La Lucille* in 1919. By now, George's brother Ira was writing the librettos, and their first Broadway success was with *Lady Be Good* in 1924. The first real smash however, that really put the Broadway musical on the map, was written by Jerome Kern and Oscar Hammerstein. *Showboat*, in 1927, set a pattern for all future musicals in America, insofar as the subject matter was exclusively about American life past and present. *Showboat* celebrated the nostalgia for the old Swanee days.

The perfect lyric for a musical should be inspired directly by the story and the characters contained in it. In fact, ideally, a song in a musical should carry on whenever the dialogue leaves off.

Oscar Hammerstein

Oklahoma would do the same for the Old West, *Guys and Dolls* for Chicago Gangsters, and *West Side Story* for teenage gang warfare in 1950s New York. Furthermore it was the diversity of Broadway that made it so rich. The first musical created by black Americans, was *Shuffle Along* in 1921, written by Eubie Blake and Noble Sissle.

By 1929, a great new singer/songwriter Fats Waller, had presented and starred in his first musical review, *Hot Chocolates*. Through jazz and musicals, blacks were making an impression… up North. Broadway could never have happened south of the Mason-Dixon Line!

By design or by accident, the stage musical together with Hollywood, would ultimately result in worldwide Americanisation.

Musical theatre in Britain seemed staid by comparison in the 1920s. Ivor Novello was still looking back, with shows like *A to Z*, which starred Jack Buchanan, Beatrice Lilley and Gertrude Lawrence, the greatest stars of the London stage. But there was a new force in town, a tour de force. He was Noel Coward, and his early musicals included *London Calling, This Year Of Grace* and *Bitter Sweet* in 1928. It was Coward's humour and pathos, so very, very English, that was to captivate America as well as Britain, with songs like *Poor Little Rich Girl*, and *Dance Little Lady*. Coward understood Broadway and youth:

> *Though you're only seventeen,*
> *Far too much of life you've seen,*
> *Syncopated child.*
> *Maybe if you only knew,*
> *Where your path was leading to*
> *You'd become less wild.*
> *But I know its vain*
> *Trying to explain*
> *While there's this insane*
> *Music in your brain.*
>
> Noel Coward, *Dance Little Lady.*

So, how to classify all this stage music, from the Ziegfeld Follies to Lloyd Webber? There is no point attempting to be clever and 'see' things that lend a supposed gravitas to what is first and foremost, popular music. Notwithstanding, the lyrics were often brilliant, witty, and above all very sophisticated. They were of their time, and for an educated audience. However, this sophistication would come to grief with an event in 1939 that I will deal with in the next chapter. It would herald the death throws of the professional Tin Pan Alley songwriters and put the 'power' firmly back in the hands of the common man, the new 'folk' musician.

In the 1920s, Hollywood was already the home of a fledgling movie industry, which started life in the Blondeau Tavern, shut by 'temperance enthusiasts', or killjoys as we would call them. The building on Sunset and Gower, was rented by the Nestor Company and became the first studio there.

After that brief history, let's talk music. Silent movies have no place in this book, for obvious reasons. However, good old Edison came up with a way of laying a soundtrack on to film, and in 1926, his company Vitaphone produced a 'short' with sound. It was the following year, that the first full-length talkie was released, and guess what, it was a musical.

The Jazz Singer had been a Broadway musical starring George Jessel, but the movie version starred a man who styled himself, modestly I feel, Mr. Entertainment, Al Jolson. *The Jazz Singer* was a global phenomenon, because the audiences could finally hear actors speak... and sing. My reasons for loving it are somewhat different. This movie exemplified all that had gone on in America in the previous 100 years, and here's how. Jolson, the star, was an Eastern European Jew. Prior to becoming a movie star, he had been a member of Christy's Minstrels, the longest running show in minstrel or any other history.

In the film, he was a 'black face' character... and the songs he sang? They were written by Irving Berlin and George Gershwin. *Swanee*, Gershwin's big hit number in the movie, was borrowed, in part, from a song written in the 1840s, *Swanee River*, by Stephen Foster. So you see, *The Jazz Singer* is a time capsule of the creativity and excitement of America's popular music from the 19th to 20th centuries. It could have been designed that way, but I bet it wasn't.

Playbill for The Beggar's Opera

Robert Walpole

Daniel Emmett

John Gay

Thomas Edison with phonograph

Emile Berliner

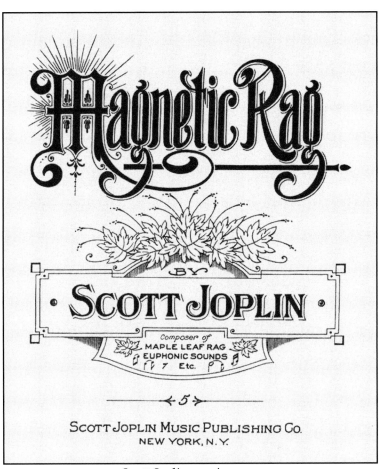

Scott Joplin music cover

*Gilbert & Sullivan poster for
Pirates of Penzance*

Enrico Caruso

W. C. Handy

The original Dixieland Jazz Band

Jelly Roll Morton

George M. Cohen (left) and Ivor Novello

James Reese Europe Band

1920s Radio

Paul Whiteman

Louis Armstrong

George Dewey Hay

Grand Ole Opry

John Philip Sousa

Irving Berlin (above)
and George Gerswin

Fats Waller

Noel Coward

Al Jolson

Bing Crosby

Woody Guthrie (above)

Leadbelly (Huddie William Ledbetter)

Robert Johnson

Cow Cow Davenport

Duke Ellington at the Hurricane Club 1943

Bob Wills and his Texas Playboys

Gene Autry

Roy Rogers

Finally let's return to radio. From there came the final piece of the musical puzzle that would lead us to the present day.

No matter how good your material is if you are a songwriter, it will rise or fall on interpretation. In the case of instrumental music, especially jazz, there is a certain amount of leeway, sometimes a hell of a lot. Extemporisation runs riot. With vocals it's a different matter. The vocalist sings the written melody, give or take a few freebies, but his or her performance will sell the song, literally.

Ex-Yale man Rudy Vallee started a band in college, and brought it to England in 1924. On returning to the States, he soon had his own radio show, which he always opened with the same words: "Heigh-ho everybody". Not original, but really friendly. The funny thing was, he sang through a megaphone... on radio.

Actually it helped to get his voice out, over the band volume. Someone said it had a keening quality, others said it was simply an aid for a weak voice. Whatever. This 'keening' sound became corrupted to 'crooning', and the Crooner was born. Rudy Vallee was first real pop singer, and he was also responsible for an indispensable aid to vocalists:

I borrowed an old carbon 'mike' from NBC, hooked up a home-made amplifier with some radios, and I got a sort of electronic megaphone.

Rudy Vallee.

Yes, in 1930, Rudy Vallee invented the PA system, without which no respectable, or otherwise, rock group could ever function. Sadly, Vallee's days as number one, were limited. All because of a man who could 'sell' songs in a much cooler manner; Bing Crosby. Crosby, son of poor Irish immigrants, formed a group, The Rhythm Boys, and sang with the Paul Whiteman band from 1926. Leaving in 1929, he got his own radio show, live from L.A's Coconut Grove. The show's theme became Bing's; *When The Blue Of The Night*. Vocal nodules gave his voice a quality not unlike 'singing into a rain barrel', his own words. He also called himself the Old Groaner. But it was, above all, his use of the recently invented microphone that set him apart from all who had gone before. He used it as if it was the one person he was singing to. The effect was wonderfully up-front and personal.

Bing Crosby taught everyone how to be cool. He wore a sweater, he played golf. He invented the art of intimate singing. He defied categories. Before Crosby there were Irish singers, jazz singers, folk singers. Crosby was an American singer.

Tony Bennett

It's the first part of that statement I have difficulties with. Since when did wearing a sweater and playing golf make someone cool? In 1930, only for a minute section of society. How many people could aspire to join a golf club, for heaven's sake?

The second part, I believe, is spot on. Crosby took all the American musical influences and moulded them into one homogeneous mixture and style, the American popular song. A yardstick by which all future singers would be measured.

8

Everybody's Doin' It

Prior to the 20th century, there had been no 'global economy' as such. True, Britain had controlled three quarters of the world, but with little or no competition, the buck stopped here.

When Wall Street crashed in 1929, the whole developed world caught a nasty cold. Depression on such a scale destroyed business and consumer confidence, and the entertainment industry was not immune.

However, some areas of the music biz remained surprisingly buoyant. It was the 'poor' end of the market that prospered, which perhaps shouldn't be a surprise at all. The people will always seek out their own music, the music they feel is representative of their situation and their struggles. In those times they turn to musicians who articulate their specific grievances.

One such case was Jimmie Rodgers, a railroad worker and occasional hobo, who became the first real country star in the late 20s. His style was an eclectic mix of blues and country, with an unusual European addition: yodelling. Actually, Jimmie borrowed this from a singer called Emmett Miller, who recorded a great song, *Lovesick Blues*, in 1924, later to be made famous by Hank Williams. But Rodger's blues/country style also included an Hawaiian guitar. You didn't 'pick' or strum this, you ran a comb or knife blade along the fretboard, on an 'open chord tuning'. This was ultimately refined to become the infamous pedal steel guitar, the mainstay of all Country music from the 1930s to the 1970s.

In 1929 a short film gave Jimmie his lasting soubriquet, *The Singing Brakeman*, which referred to his earlier career. With songs like *Pistol Packing Papa, In The Jailhouse Now* and *Muleskinner Blues,* Jimmie's records were million sellers during a career that only lasted five years. But how could this happen during a depression? The answer is that Jimmie was perceived to be 'one of us' by the poor, and when they were shopping for the meagre necessities of life, they felt duty bound to include a Jimmie Rodgers record with the groceries! Rodgers was a template for all future country singers, and the only one who could boast of having the great Louis Armstrong play on one of his records, *Blue Yodel No.9*. He died in 1933 after a lifelong struggle with TB.

What is interesting here is that while commercial and sophisticated music suffered in the Depression, the simple, folksy music of the people flourished. This, I believe, is the key to understanding the importance of the popular song. By its very nature, pop is regarded by many people as peripheral and easily disposable. But equally many others regard it as an essential part of every day life. Of course there are often crossovers that please an all- encompassing audience, but in the main the difference can be found in the lyrics. Trite, banal, sing-along, dance-along words that make up fifty percent of many pop songs, are inconsequential to fan and critic alike. But the lyrics of a true folk/country, down-home tune resonate with the ordinary man, and have done from the days of the minstrels right up to Bob Dylan, Johnny Cash, Garth Brooks and their ilk.

Am I suggesting a two tier pop industry? Actually no: I have made some cringingly commercial records and some classic hits, but it would be entirely wrong, not to mention impossible, to attempt to make a clear artistic distinction. To do so would cause total confusion. How, you would ask, could Dylan have written both *Blowin' In The Wind* and *Mighty Quinn*? The latter is one of my hits, and the lyrics are nonsense, but I am happy to say it is still heard today far more frequently than the former. All this means is that Bob Dylan is a songwriter who writes as the mood takes him, without constraint. He would probably hate to be classified as a pop writer, but that's exactly what he is, albeit one with the talent to communicate poetically and commercially, not necessarily at the same time. Perhaps there would never have been a Dylan without the emergence of another great folk singer/songwriter in the 1930s.

Woody Guthrie started with a few disadvantages. His father went bankrupt, his mother was committed to a mental home, his sister was killed and he himself suffered from Huntington's Chorea, a progressive wasting disease for which there is no cure. A self-taught man and a self confessed socialist, Guthrie wrote some of the greatest folk songs of his and any other generation. Songs like *This Land Is Your Land, Pastures Of Plenty,* and *This Train Is Bound For Glory* were songs for the common man. His Dust Bowl Ballads, a homage to the dirt farmers of Kansas during the Depression, were recorded by the great American folk archivist Alan Lomax for the Library of Congress. This sat uncomfortably alongside Guthrie's membership of the Communist Party of America, and his pieces in the American *Daily Worker* newspaper. There is no question he was a zealot. His guitar bore the inscription: 'This machine kills fascists'.

This now begs the question; does politics belong in pop music? You may as well ask does pop music belong in politics. The answer to both is a resounding yes. It always has and it always will: no more no less than love, angst, humour, and the entire gamut of emotions. The singer/songwriter is no less an observer of the human condition than the poet and author, and in many cases they can touch the soul far more directly and accurately than many learned scribes.

Just as folk and country singers were evolving and crossing over, so the blues was going through the same metamorphosis. It had certainly been around in one shape or another since the first half of the 19th century. From the white blues of Kentucky to the 'field hollers' of plantation slaves, with a dose of traditional folk melodies thrown in, this basic 12 bar 'do it yourself' music was beginning to sizzle.

In the 1920s, Ma Rainey and Bessie Smith had 'jazzed up' country blues and apart from the 'bent' vocal notes, it had become almost indistinguishable from New Orleans jazz. However, by the 1930s the Mississippi Delta had spawned a new crop of blues singers, and a new, rougher style of the blues, far more akin to the work songs of the old South. Huddy Leadbetter, known as Leadbelly, spent a good part of his life in prison from 1918 onwards. However, his music stood him in good stead. Both in 1925 and 1934, this 'sweet singer from the swamplands', gained pardons from life sentences by writing songs to the State Governors! In his case music certainly was 'the food of life'.

Many of these blues singers had moved to the cities and gave voice to their discontent and marginalisation through their music. One of the first of these was Charlie Patton. He played straight and bottleneck guitar, and sang everything from blues to folk and pop. Along with Son House and Leadbelly, he was the inspiration for the likes of Muddy Waters, Howlin' Wolf, and certainly that most legendary of all bluesmen, Robert Johnson.

The reason Johnson attained such cult status, probably owes more to Faust than any twelve bar opus. The story goes that Johnson was playing with Son House in 1930, and then disappeared for a few weeks. What is alleged to have happened during that time has become the stuff of music legend. Johnson is said to have met the Devil at a crossroads, and fought a musical duel with him. If Johnson lost, his soul would be forfeit, but if he won his 'prize' was to play guitar better than anyone!

Robert Johnson's 'victory' has been celebrated in movies and song ever since, not least in his own classic, *Crossroads*.

Son House said there was definitely something strange going on because when Johnson turned up again, his guitar playing was far better than it had been.

Now call me a cynic, but I am not too keen on this theory. It was good old fashioned PR, that would not be out of place today in *Pop Idol*. Anything that gives a performer an edge is utilised in the great struggle for success, and the Devil is as good if not better than most; and it worked. Even Johnson's passing was linked to the 'black arts', although it was rather more sordid. He was poisoned by a jilted husband in 1938... but it was all a part of Mississippi Delta folk lore whichever way you look at it. Things were somewhat more businesslike up North.

In New York's Tin Pan Alley, writers experienced an avatar, or rather, a 'second coming' in the early 30s. In their early days, the Alleymen churned out sweet, often mindless little ditties to feed the masses, but the songwriting qualities of the new bunch were out of this world. I suppose superb sophistication is the best way of describing works by Kern, Porter, Hoagy Carmichael, George and Ira Gershwin, and the rest of the 'golden boys' in the 1930s. Downright bloody genius would be better!

To be sure, it was the Golden Age of Song. The fact that pop had now turned into an industry, was the key. Records, radio, technology, and Hollywood were driving entertainment like never before. Pop was now big business, and it needed big songs and big bands. Besides, prohibition had ended in 1933, and the world was coming out of depression. Enthusiasm was the order of the day:

First of all let me assert my firm belief that the only thing we have to fear is fear itself.
President Franklin Delano Roosevelt, 1933

In the 1920s Paul Whiteman had pioneered the 'big band', but it was really an orchestra, and the antithesis of hot jazz.

What happened in the early 1930s was that big bands began to be 'cool'. This was largely due to musical arrangers, like Don Redman, who wrote parts for horns (trumpets) and reed sections (saxophones), as if they were soloists. Redman had originally worked with the Fletcher Henderson band in the 1920s, and therefore had been inspired by Louis Armstrong's style of playing. The real big band era erupted around 1935 with clarinettist Benny Goodman's band playing artfully arranged pieces, written by the likes of Henderson.

What followed was the Swing Era. What was Swing apart from four beats to the bar rather than two, as in Dixieland Jazz?

Arrangers like Redman found huge success by writing notations that were slightly behind the beat, or in some cases ahead of it. It was all in the phrasing. This 'phrasing' had come from the original jazz greats, not least Armstrong, who stretched his solos across the beat, and bent the notes beautifully. This of course, was the essence of jazz and the blues, and was quintessentially black driven. As this new swing music took off, it was the white bands, however, which prospered. Black musicians were not allowed to play in 'whites' only hotels and clubs, and some went to great lengths to circumnavigate this musical apartheid.

Duke Ellington, one of the greatest jazz composers and arrangers, powdered his hair and face in order to look more 'white', and therefore be able to play in restricted venues. What price Michael Jackson in the 1990s?

Whatever the problems, swing, black and white, was king. The best black bands, Ellington, Lunceford, and Redman, stood alongside the best white bands of Tommy Dorsey, Artie Shaw, and the most popular of all, Glen Miller. American kids were 'jitterbugging' or jiving to all of them, black and white, and talking the 'talk'; jive talk. In 1936, Benny Goodman played five concerts in one day at New York's Paramount Theatre, starting at 10.30 in the morning! The queues went round the block, and 200,000 turned up for a Swing bash at Chicago's Soldiers Field Stadium that same year. *Time* magazine likened it to:

The Children's Crusade of medieval times

If it was a crusade, its leader was undoubtedly John Hammond, Jr. He was the legendary producer of many famous bands, and the real champion of Swing, presenting a series of concerts at New York's Carnegie Hall in 1938. Called *From Spirituals To Swing*, it included ex-taxi driver Albert Ammons playing a piano driven blues style, heavy on the left hand, called Boogie Woogie. Boogie was the 'child' of the Barrelhouse piano style from the 1890s, and had been pioneered by the wonderfully named Cow Cow Davenport, and Clarence 'Pinetop' Smith. The story goes that Hammond tried to book Robert Johnson for the concerts, but unfortunately the poison beat him to it!

Swing was 'the thing', and even country and western music was not immune! Texan Bob Wills formed his Texas Playboys around 1935. The band consisted of Bob on fiddle, guitars, rhythm section, trombone, sax, and a pedal steel guitar, an instrument used commercially for the first time in country or any other musical genre. It was quite an eclectic mix, but the Texas Playboys would grow to become a 21-piece band! Their many hits were produced by an Englishman, Art Satherley. Art also produced Gene Autry, and various legendary blues artistes. He is the only Englishman to be inducted into the Country Music Hall Of Fame.

Not bad for a Bristol boy who ran away to the USA aged 17, joined Thomas Edison's company, and then became a talent scout for Victor Records.

Swing was educated jazz with dashes of the blues, played superbly, but above all arranged immaculately, and it was pure pop. Much of it however, was purely instrumental. There were great singers like Bing Crosby, Peggy Lee, and Ella Fitzgerald, and vocal groups like the Mills Brothers, whose close harmonies were based on band arrangements, not to mention barber shop quartets; and the audiences loved them, because they could identify with them! But swing had yet to find its true voice, literally.

The man who was probably the first great pop singer/songwriter, was Fats Waller. From writing Broadway reviews, like *Hot Chocolates* in the 1920s, and selling songs to the likes of Fletcher Henderson for hamburgers (really), Fats had become a big success by the 1930s. He wrote 63 hits, 38 making number one in the song charts. Many of his songs were humorous like *Your Feet's Too Big*:

Your pedal extremities really are obnoxious!

Others were simply classics: *Lulu's Back In Town, I'm Gonna Sit Right Down And Write Myself A Letter,* and *Two Sleepy People.* Of the 800 or so songs Fats wrote, less than 70 remained in his ownership on the day he died. The rest had been given away in return for meals and general sustenance, or purloined by dishonest music publishers.

Tin Pan Alley songwriters had no such problems. Theirs was a well-regulated business, almost a nine to five existence, and they had two stairways to royalties heaven, Hollywood and Broadway. In 1933 Warner Brothers gave a shot in the arm to movie musicals by releasing the Al Dubin and Harry Warren show, *42nd Street.* Two years later, George Gershwin hit Broadway with possibly his best musical, *Porgy and Bess,* and what a score it was. He gained his inspiration from spending time down South and listening to the Gullah Negroes in South Carolina. The result was a musical triumph, and a deliberate crossover of classic Broadway, and the blues.

Hollywood was also churning out B movie Westerns with amazing rapidity. One of its biggest stars was Gene Autry who, not content with bringing the bad guys to justice and winning the hands of various pretty girls, also carried a guitar and sang to his horse. The singing cowboy became big business, and like his forefather, the Minstrel, sang the songs of the people... well, Western people to be exact. Autrey was possibly also the first 'guitar hero' since

Casanova! During World War 2 his place would be taken by an even more famous cowboy star, Roy Rogers.

Back East, England to be exact, our home-grown music was still in a bit of a time warp. Yes, we had our own jazz bands like Henry Hall and Jack Hylton, but they were rather British and conservative. But what was very British were the musicals and the popular singers.

Songwriter Noel Gay wrote the classic show *Me And My Girl*, which showcased such greats as *Leaning On A Lamp-Post*, and *The Lambeth Walk*. The former became a huge hit for a nasally challenged Lancashire lad, George Formby. With his little banjo-ukelele, George sang tunes laced with innuendo like *When I'm Cleaning Windows* and *Little Stick Of Blackpool Rock*. The BBC was embarrassed but the public loved 'our George', right down to his bad teeth and gormless face. He was real, he was from Wigan for heaven's sake!

George's female equivalent was also from Lancashire. Gracie Fields could belt songs out in a mock operatic voice, or do comedy point numbers. The same innuendo was still there: who actually had *The Biggest Aspidestra In The World*? You had to wonder. The newspapers didn't wonder, they were convinced:

She captures the spirit of good humour and optimism that alone has prevented the depressed and dispossessed in smitten industrial areas from succumbing to the tragedies surrounding them.
Birmingham Mail, 1934

The British were much in evidence in the 1930s, but really only in Britain, with a very few exceptions. Jack Buchanan and Jessie Matthews starred in the odd Hollywood movie, and Broadway musical, and Noel Coward was the toast of the American nightclub circuit. But then as far as America was concerned, they were typically English; snooty, upper crust English. The 'real' English were Formby, 'our Gracie', and Flanagan and Allen, but you couldn't sell it to the Yanks, they couldn't even understand them. Actually, George was singing a variation of ragtime, and Gracie was locked in somewhere between the Victorian and Edwardian eras. Regardless, they were our two biggest stars of the 1930s, and so what if America didn't 'get it'? They didn't 'get' Cliff Richard either.

Gracie Fields was Britain, she was an example, and George Formby was her spiritual husband, and the best banjo-ukelele player in the world.

Ian Whitcomb, *After The Ball*

Our Gracie ended up marrying an Italian Prince and living on the Isle of Capri in abject luxury. So typically British, don't you think?

So why the great difference between American dynamism and British conservatism? Well, the immediate difference in the 1930s was obvious: we were at the end of empire, whilst the Americans were already the richest nation on earth, shortly to reach superpower status. But there was more to it. Immigrants had given the USA a tremendous vitality and diversity in many areas, not least entertainment. We were still insular, relying on the tried and trusted, the sort of things we were used to and felt comfortable with. But most of all it was the beginning of globalisation, and it was American-driven globalisation. By the close of the 1930s, young Europeans would be immersed in a hamburger, juke joint, drive-in culture, courtesy of Hollywood, even though it would be 25 years before this manifested itself.

Funnily enough, the French were slightly more at home with the Jazz and Swing ages. This was because notable black American musicians like Sidney Bechet took up residence in France, in protest at racial intolerance back home. Indeed, the French took to jazz, calling it, with typical French un-cool, Le Jazz Hot. They probably also thought they had a hand in inventing it. After all, Louisiana was originally French!

The first great European jazz musicians were Django Reinhardt, a Belgian who lived in France, and Stefan Grapelli, a Frenchman with an Italian name. It has to be said that their particular brand of jazz owed more to European supper clubs than the exciting jazz sounds of New Orleans and New York. But at least it was their own, unlike the ersatz British bands. But Europe and Britain in particular, had more to think about than pop music as the 1930s drew to a close.

In America, Bessie Smith, the Empress of the Blues, died in a car accident in 1937, having been refused admission to a segregated hospital in Memphis, and the new Queen of the Blues was Billie Holiday. Named Lady Day by great saxophonist and mentor Lester

Young, Billie was adored and deified by musicians, but only found true fame after her death, probably because she was a great stylist rather than a great singer. Her recording of *Strange Fruit,* adapted from a Lewis Allen poem about Negro lynchings in the South, is still her greatest epitaph.

So as the 1930s drew to a close, where were we in terms of pop? Well, jazz had become pop with swing and the big bands. Blues had also crossed over into jazz, as had country to swing. Still on their own 'straight and narrow', were the urban blues, folk music and country. What was not obvious then, was that these three seemingly diverse music forms, were about to collide and merge, into rock n' roll.

In 1939 the world was about to change, for the worse. Music was also about to change, but would it be for better or for worse? That would all depend on your age.

9

One For My Baby

1939, and Europe was at war. London was preparing for possible invasion, and probable bombing. The music halls were packed to hear Flanagan and Allen poke fun at Hitler with songs like *We're Going To Hang Out The Washing On The Siegfried Line* and *Run Rabbit Run*. How typical of the Brits to laugh and sing while standing on the edge of a precipice, looking down:

> *We're going to hang out the washing on the Siegfried Line,*
> *If the Siegfried Line's still there!*

In America, they looked on in some confusion at the wretched Europeans, at it again only 20 years after the last holocaust. There, all was still light and fun, not least the sounds of swinging big bands. While the world held its breath, two events occurred in the States, neither of which was earth shattering, but both of which would change popular music forever.

A few years earlier, the American trade organisation that collected money for songwriters and publishers, from radio station airplay, ASCAP (American Society for Authors, Composers and Publishers), had demanded a whopping increase from all the radio stations. Most of the big ones agreed, but some held out, and ASCAP members went on strike in late 1940. This meant that ALL the great Alley writers from Berlin to Rodgers, withdrew their music from public performance.

To counter this move, 256 small stations had formed an alternative to ASCAP. Called BMI, Broadcast Music Incorporated, the only music this new outfit could attract, was the kind of stuff the big boys had no interest in: poor white and black music. Even some publishers switched to BMI, notably those involved with the 'alternative' markets: blues and country.

These 'minority' styles of music, would now be heard by larger numbers of people, many of whom were definitely of the 'younger generation'. They didn't know it, but they were on the road to Rock n' Roll.

As a nation, the United States has long been unduly modest in matters of the arts. At present, we are one of the most musical nations in the world. The most vital, most original music being written today, is American music. Up to the present time you have been able to hear in public, and to buy for your own use, the music of none but a comparatively small group of writers. The established publishing houses have preferred to deal only with established writers. BMI has dropped the bars, and now the new men, the young men, the men you have not known, can bring you their songs.
                                                                BMI announcement, 1940

By now, America was the richest country on earth, and the middle classes were already 'living the dream': wide open spaces, big cars, Hollywood, home ownership, money. Their children were no exception. Pocket money gave them a spending power never before available to youngsters anywhere on the planet. This made them a target, in marketing terms, for big business, and music was in the vanguard.

The original crooners, Rudy Vallee and Bing Crosby, held no fascination for this new generation, and the big band leaders were beginning to realise this. Hollywood had already dictated that its heroes and heroines should look perfect in every way, with perfect hair, perfect teeth, and a perfect lifestyle. Swing bands, led by great musicians like Glen Miller and Artie Shaw, looked like a motley collection of bank managers and accountants. What did they care? Their music spoke for them, not their haircuts. One of these bandleaders, Tommy Dorsey, thought otherwise, when he signed an up and coming, young singer, to front his band in 1940.

Francis Albert Sinatra had been singing with the Harry James band for a few months, when someone suggested to Dorsey that he hire 'the skinny kid who sings with Harry's band'. Within one year Sinatra had become the top male band vocalist in the USA, displacing Crosby in *Downbeat* magazine's poll, in 1941. Crosby's famous line said it all:

Frank Sinatra is the kind of singer that comes along once in a lifetime: why did it have to be my lifetime?

Bing Crosby, 1941

You know what he meant. In any era, Bing would have been a successful performer, but Frankie? He was a megastar in the making; a 'one off'. His timing, in singing and business, was impeccable. As World War 2 drew to a close, the big bands would cease to be fashionable, leaving the field open to the solo singer. Sinatra was extremely prescient on this point, buying himself out of his contract with Tommy Dorsey in 1941.

His girl fans were termed 'bobbysoxers' after their cute white tennis socks. Soon, a catch-all generic term would be coined to describe his fans: teenagers. Frank Sinatra was the very first teenage idol, which was clear when, in 1944, he appeared at New York's Paramount Theatre, and 25,000 screaming teenagers, queued round the block to buy tickets. He had the pre-requisite Latin features, a mandatory requirement since the days of silent movie star Rudolf Valentino; he was a skinny kid who looked like he needed mothering; and when he sang, you knew he was singing just for you. The great thing to understand about Sinatra, was that he was not, and never had been, a jazz singer. First and foremost he was a pop singer, albeit a very exceptional one. He was something special. Just as Louis Armstrong was the face of jazz, Frank was the face of swing. He was also something else, essential to the young; he was cool. But he was still a Tin Pan Alley product, in that he had the greatest writers to provide him with material, at the greatest level of sophistication. What he didn't know, was that something was brewing in other, less sophisticated parts of the USA, and that 'something' would ultimately eclipse him, the Alley, and swing, completely; and the driving force behind that change would be the very age-group that created him: the teenagers.

In the 1940s, Hollywood musicals were beginning to be big business. Sinatra starred in several himself, like *Anchors Aweigh* and *On The Town*. Musicals were vehicles for the great writers of the 1920s and 30s, with an extra magic ingredient: the American

79

Dream. They nearly all started life as Broadway shows, and the biggest stars of the Great White Way were Rodgers and Hart; and who could argue with such a pedigree?

A Connecticut Yankee (*My Heart Stood Still*); *Spring Is Here* (*With A Song In My Heart*); *Evergreen* (*Dancing On The Ceiling*); *Present Arms* (*You Took Advantage Of Me*); *On Your Toes* (*There's A Small Hotel*); *Babes In Arms* (*Where Or When, Lady Is A Tramp, I Wish I Were In Love Again*); *Pal Joey* (*I Could Write A Book, Bewitched Bothered and Bewildered*).

On the death of Lorenz Hart, Rodgers replaced him with a new partner, Oscar Hammerstein II, a librettist more interested in operetta than swing influenced pop. Thus together they wrote: *Oklahoma!* (*Oh What A Beautiful Morning, People Will Say We're In Love*); *Carousel* (*You'll Never Walk Alone, If I Loved You*); *South Pacific* (*Gonna Wash That Man Right Outa My Hair, Some Enchanted Evening*); *The King and I* (*Hello Young Lovers*); *State Fair* (*It Might As Well Be Spring*); and *Flower Drum Song* (*I Enjoy Being A Girl*); and finally, the most successful screen musical of all time, *The Sound Of Music*.

As a rule I am not too keen on lists, but with credits like Rodgers, Hart and Hammerstein's, it had to be done. In the field of stage and screen musicals, they reigned and will always reign supreme. Sorry Andrew and Tim, but there it is; and to prove the point, if that were necessary, please allow me to quote the lyrics of the great Lorenz Hart:

> *When love congeals,*
> *It soon reveals,*
> *The faint aroma of performing seals,*
> *The double crossing of a pair of heels,*
> *I wish I were in love again.*

It's poetry, nothing less, and the English is superb, right down to the grammatically correct 'were in love again'. It is also a dying art. Perhaps it's already dead. How sad.

In the 1940s, other music styles were light years away from the sophistication of Richard Rodgers and friends. This did not make them any less important: in fact in the light of what was to come, they were _more_ important.

The gospel music of Thomas Dorsey, had become the driving 'blues' tinged gospel of Mahalia Jackson and Sister Rosetta Tharpe. You only have to listen to Tharpe's *This Train Is Bound For Glory*, to hear some of rock n' roll's roots. She had come from the pop/jazz side of the business, originally singing with Cab Calloway. But her electric guitar solos were way ahead of their time, evoking shades of Bonny Raitt today. Her songs like *Up Above My Head* were covered by 1950s hitmakers Frankie Laine and Johnnie Ray.

While Bob Wills and his Texas Playboys were swinging, Bill Monroe was staying true to his roots. Those roots were Bluegrass; Kentucky music, that remained fairly true to its British ancestry. The high, keening wail set up by Monroe would not have seemed out of place in Lincolnshire or Oxfordshire in the 18th century. He sang what he referred to as 'true songs', that is the songs of his ancestors. Furthermore his band included Lester Flatt and Earl Scruggs, the best banjo picker on earth. Monroe also wrote *Blue Moon Of Kentucky*, which would turn out to be the 'B' side of Elvis' first single in 1954.

Woody Guthrie had now teamed up with another folk legend, Pete Seeger. Pete suffered from the same problem Woody did: misplaced political orientation. He was a communist in the greatest capitalist state on earth. The Almanac Singers also included Lee Hays and Millard Lampell, and they had their work cut out to succeed. World War 2 broke up the group, and in 1946 Seeger started a series of People's Concerts called 'hootenannies', a word he is said to have found in Seattle. As McCarthyism loomed left wing Pete Seeger would be on a hiding to nothing, until he formed a new group, the Weavers in the 1950s.

Perhaps the most enjoyable form of 'alternative' music in the 1940s, was Rhythm n' Blues. A hybrid comprising swing, blues and boogie, it was the natural follow up to the music of the big bands. The dances associated with R&B were the also the same: jitterbugging and jiving. The big difference was in the number of participating musicians. Gone were the big arranged horn and brass sections, and in came the small combo.

The premiere R&B outfit was the Tympany Five, led by Louis Jordan. Jordan still dallied with jazz and swing, backing star names from Crosby to Ella Fitzgerald, but he knew he was on to something big. He wrote hits like *Choo Choo Ch'Boogie*, and *There Ain't Nobody Here But Us Chickens*, and is remembered to this day in a musical celebrating his music called *Five Guys Named Mo*. Sadly for Louis, he missed the boat. He was signed to Decca Records, and produced by Milt Gabler, but left him in the early 1950s due to artistic differences. Gabler almost immediately signed a replacement R&B group, called Bill Haley and the Saddlemen. It was the birth of rock n' roll, which poor old Louis Jordan had started, unwittingly, ten years before.

I cannot leave the 1940s without mentioning one other name. Just as Louis Jordan influenced the coming rock revolution, so did Hank Williams, a young Alabama country boy. Like his predecessor Jimmie Rodgers, Hank was an accident waiting to happen. In Hank's case it was spina bifida that set him on a rocky road to nowhere through alcohol abuse. In his very short life, he wrote the template for many hit songs of the 50s and 60s. In 1948, for example, his song *Move It On Over*, was a 'note for note' pre-cursor to *Rock Around The Clock*, whilst in the 1950s, such luminaries as Frankie Laine, Tony Bennett and Jo Stafford, recorded many of his songs, such as *Cold Cold Heart, Jambalaya, Half As Much* and *Your Cheating Heart*. Jazz snobbery was very much in evidence, when Bennett refused, at first, to do *Cold Cold Heart*. What a sap. It became a number one for him 1951.

> *I tried so hard my dear, to show that you're my every dream*
> *Yet you're afraid each thing I do, is just some evil scheme*
> *A memory from your lonesome past, keeps us so far apart,*
> *Why can't I free your doubtful mind,*
> *And melt your cold, cold heart.*
> Hank Williams, *Cold, Cold Heart*

In the 1960s, blues great Ray Charles recorded many Williams songs on his classic album, Modern Sounds In Country and Western. In the 1970s, the Carpenters and many others continued to use his material.

All this has made Hank Williams the greatest star in Country Music's history, and it has been said that, but for lack of drumming in his band, he could have been the first rock n' roll singer in the world. His life style also followed suit: failed marriages, fights, drugs (painkillers), and alcoholism. He died aged 29, in 1953. Baby, that's Rock n' Roll.

So, look at the 1940s. The teenager was 'born', assisted by the legendary Frank Sinatra. Original jazz had already metamorphasised into that thing called Swing, pop by any other name. The really serious afficionados were going for a new 'jump' beat style pioneered by Charlie Parker and Dizzy Gillespie, called Be-Bop. The name, incidentally, is said to come from Gillespie's 'scat singing', the vocal instrumental noises that tortured the epiglottis, not to mention the average listener. Like the new big band style of Stan Kenton, that appeared to be a cacophony of mindless noise to many, and would ultimately become Modern Jazz, these two styles of music were not pop, as both fans and detractors would be only too happy to confirm.

Most of the old big bands had fallen by the wayside to be replaced by smaller rhythm and blues combos, the forerunners of the classic rock n' roll line-up. Country music had also gone 'pop', through Hank Williams, and Broadway/Hollywood musicals had gone in the opposite direction, continuing the Tin Pan Alley tradition of the journeymen songwriters like Rodgers and Hammerstein. And folk? Well, that was as it had ever been, a law unto itself, but still rooted in the music of the common man. British music was virtually non-existent, and let's face it, there was a very good reason. World War 2 had bankrupted us, and finished off the Empire for good. We had more to think about, like a health service and employment, rather than luxuries like entertainment and popular music. Besides, we still had the odd Ivor Novello revival, and Noel Coward's wit, but mostly we just tagged along behind our American cousins, copying their music and losing ourselves in a technicolour Hollywood world; a world of multi-ethnicity, and diverse musical strands.

Now those disparate strands would quickly converge, aided and abetted first by technology, in a decade that started with the ubiquitous 78 rpm record and ended with the 33⅓ rpm long playing record, and which saw the emergence of a youth market. However, this youth market would be very different from the 'bobbysoxer' fans of Sinatra. They would be rebels, with or without a cause!

10

Sweet Little Sixteen

America: 1950s.

I love the 1950s. Most people of a certain age regard the 1960s as the 'big one', the most exciting time in pop, especially in Britain; but not me. Yes, I'll admit the 60s was a wonderful time to be young and creative, and most certainly it was a time when anything and everything seemed attainable: but it was all made possible by the events of the 1950s, and the inexorable march of youth. The new 'Cold War' and the threat of a nuclear holocaust would provide the impetus throughout Europe for protest. The Un-American Activities Committee, under Senator McCarthy would turn friend against friend in Hollywood and Washington, and leave its mark on the music business. The Iron Curtain; segregation in the American Southern States; food shortages in Europe; these things were all perceived, rightly or wrongly, as problems caused by the War generation, the older generation. There was an unspoken feeling that only youth, the 'new guard', could lead the way to a better world. That is why the 1950s were so exciting. They were really the formative years, the rehearsal for the liberated swinging 60s.

Pop in the USA was mush in the early 1950s, with stars like Jo Stafford and Doris Day, both ex-band singers, leading the way. Actually it was just starting to feel old fashioned, and in America that almost amounts to a death sentence. But it was still driven by a vibrant live theatre circuit, and the amazing success of the juke joints. By 1952 there were over half a million juke boxes in circulation; one for every 300 Americans! In that same year came the first broadcast on national TV of the longest running pop show in history, *American Bandstand*, presented and devised by disc jockey Dick Clark. Initially, the music was still mush, but *Bandstand* would come to be a driving force for a new teenage sound.

An interesting, if strange development, was that of 'New York' country and western singers, which sounds like a contradiction in terms! CBS Records head of A&R (artistes and repertoire), Mitch Miller, had decided that he could commercialise what he thought of as 'hick' country music, by nurturing new big voiced talent. Frankie Laine led the way, singing endless pseudo cowboy ballads and film themes. Another was Guy Mitchell, a handsome, hard drinking merchant seaman. Miller produced a string of hits for him with improbable titles like *She Wears Red Feathers (and a Hula Hula skirt)*. One of the better acts was Tennessee Ernie Ford, who recorded classics like *16 Tons*, a real country song, from a real country singer/ songwriter, Merle Travis. Travis, and his ilk knew where they belonged; south of the Mason-Dixon Line. One exception was Tex Ritter, a proper cowboy star, with a wonderful gravel voice. Even though Laine covered his hits, Tex occasionally made it through with his own records, notably *High Noon*.

Unlike Britain, however, there were some bright spots on the horizon. Johnnie Ray, a partially deaf singer who was helped by black rhythm n' blues artiste LaVern Baker, had some soul. He proved it by crying, sort of, on some of his records. This outbreak of emotion incensed the music press and *cognascenti*, thus assuring Johnnie of success. It also embarrassed Columbia Records, Mitch Miller, who, in keeping with the McCarthy era's puritanical ethos, was only interested in promoting squeaky clean, white pop singers. It is interesting to note that Miller, made his own records as an orchestra leader. His biggest was *Yellow Rose Of Texas*, a song inspired, as it turns out, by a mulatto mistress of the Mexican General Santa Anna, who destroyed the Alamo in Texas. She was known as the 'Yellow Rose', due to her colour. Mitch Miller, the scourge of common, rough edged music and musicians, was oblivious to the fact that he was glorifying a non-white hooker in his very own hit record! He had no idea, and he was quite ignorant of all the early ragtime, jazz and blues records that had gone before, as evidenced by the following quote:

Rock and roll's appeal to youngsters is the equivalent of those 'Confidential' magazines to adults. This is the first time in the history of our business that records have capitalized on illiteracy and bad recording.

Mitch Miller, 1957

And this from the man who was the brains behind such classics as *Where Will The Baby's Dimple Be*, and *She Wears Red Feathers*. But then he was consistent. Miller swore Columbia would never sign a rock act while he was there. They never did, which is why they had no great success until after his departure... in 1962. They were the only company to actually miss the 'rocking' boat completely.

However, I do believe that Johnnie Ray's emotion and energy were seminal influences on a young man from Tupelo, Mississippi, Elvis Presley. This all seems to have been ignored by those who blithely say, Presley 'stole' the black man's music. They point to the original record of *Hound Dog*, by black R&B singer Big Mama Thornton, as if to prove their point. But who wrote the song? Two new Tin Pan Alley writers, straight out of the Brill Building, both Jewish and white, Jerry Leiber and Mike Stoller. They picked up where the great writers of the 1930s and 40s left off. They found their creative home with an up and coming record label, Atlantic, which specialised in black rhythm and blues artistes. Atlantic Records was run by two Turks, Ahmet and Nesui Ertegun, who had perceived an 'opening' or gap in the market place, for black R&B groups to be brought into the mainstream. This was not going to be easy. White American kids loved R&B, but they appeared to want it from white groups!

Radio stations are falling over themselves to play the Georgia Gibbs version of 'Tweedle Dee', while listeners aren't given a chance to hear the original by LaVern Baker. Consequently, Georgia Gibbs has the hit.
Jerry Wexler, Atlantic executive/producer.

The real reason behind this state of affairs, was that the major companies were operating as a cartel, protecting their major artistes and their balance sheets from minority influences. For 'minority', read black. In the early 1950s, many states were split along segregationist lines, and major black stars like Nat King Cole, were being pulled off stage at some less than friendly southern venues. It was going to be a hard battle, but Atlantic and their black artistes, would ultimately reap their just rewards; but not until the 1960s.

Leiber and Stoller would become the most successful songwriting partnership since Rodgers and Hart. Sure, their songs were simple and crude, compared to the writers from the Golden Age; but they came out of the same mould; they were of their time, and could articulate the energy and feelings of the time. Black groups like the Clovers, the Dominoes, and most of all the Coasters, were the vehicles for Lieber and Stoller songs, but the best was yet to come.

You find me a white boy, who can sing like a black man and who doesn't wear a sweaty work shirt, and I'll show you a million dollars

Jerry Wexler, Atlantic Records

What we are talking about here is mostly style, as opposed to music. A revolution by any other name.

This revolution started fairly innocuously around 1951, when Bill Haley, and his western swing band, the Saddlemen, were recording for the Essex record label. The band included the mandatory pedal steel guitar, and they were pretty un-hip. Things changed however, when Bill decided to liven things up a little by including R&B songs in their repertoire. He took a 1948 song by the Treniers, called *Rock This Joint, Rocket 88*, a Jackie Brenston song, and changed the name of the band to the Comets, a strictly non-country soubriquet. Their first big hit was *Crazy Man, Crazy* in 1953, and lo, Rock n' Roll was born.

We're gonna tear down the ceiling,
Rip up the floor,
Smash all the windows,
And knock down the door,
We're gonna rock, rock this joint tonight
Rock This Joint, 1952

It was a product of rhythm and blues mixed with country: black and white music. Bill's music utilised the 'jive talk' of black America and hip white kids, but still maintained the straight western swing/ jazz approach. For heaven's sake, he was 30 years old and sported a ridiculous kiss-curl on his forehead to hide a receding hairline! The music was aimed at the kids, but played by comparative 'oldies'. Marlon Brando had set the scene, so to speak, with his portrayal of a Hells Angel in the 1952 cult movie, *The Wild Ones*, but his character was about as far removed from Haley's Comets as Senator McCarthy!

What do you have to rebel about? (character in bar)
Waddya got? (Marlon Brando)
Marlon Brando, *The Wild Ones*, 1952

The 'rebel without a cause' was born; before anyone had heard of James Dean, and the image was set in stone. The real genesis of rock arrived when Bill Haley recorded *Rock Around The Clock* in 1954, for American Decca. It wasn't a hit, but fate took a hand when it was used as the theme song for the teenage delinquent movie *Blackboard Jungle,* in 1955. It was this movie that really kick-started the whole teenage rebellion thing. *Rock Around The Clock* was a harmless pop song, which nonetheless carried a lethal message to the older generation; we've arrived, and things are never going to be the same again. Damn it, we'll even stay up all night!

When the clock strikes 12, we'll cool off, then
Start rocking round the clock again,
We're gonna rock rock rock around the clock tonight
Rock Around The Clock, 1954

It was Haley's only number one record, and the new 'Puritans' went wild. Rock n' Roll was the music of the Devil: it was a euphemism for sex, under-age at that: it would destroy the moral fibre of white American youth. Most teenagers knew this was crap. They only had to look at two 20th century world wars, McCarthyism, and the nuclear stand-off between the USA and Soviet Union. If these hadn't destroyed moral fibre, how on earth could pop music? What the Puritans really meant, was that teenagers had no rights, and that's how it should stay. You could die for your country, but you couldn't vote: you had no voice: you were not allowed to take decisions. Well, to hell with that. Rebellion was in the air, and the not-so subliminal message was, 'rock and roll will set you free'.

As I have already said, Haley had no image. He was a throwback to the big band era, and as such completely 'square'. The music was great, but there was something missing.

In Memphis, Tennessee, that 'something' was about to take the world by storm. Elvis Aaron Presley cut his first record at Sun Studios in 1954. He was 19 years old, and a part-time truck driver, but he looked like a god.

He affected a totally different approach to dress, favouring the Southern black garish style, along with a 'Tony Curtis' ducktail, greased and sweptback, hair-do. While cutting a record for his mother, in Sun Studios, Memphis, he was fooling around with two musicians, Scotty Moore and Bill Black, when something clicked. The studio owner, Sam Phillips, suddenly heard something that fascinated him. Presley was singing a black rhythm n' blues song, *That's Alright Mama*, with a slight country approach. Then he sang a white Bill Monroe number, *Blue Moon Of Kentucky*, with a touch of R&B. Phillips knew he'd struck the mother lode. Sam piled a 'delayed' echo on his voice, and Scotty Moore's guitar, a technique already popularised by middle-of-the-road guitar star, Les Paul, and he released the tracks, which were received well locally. The urgency of Presley's vocals, the overt sexiness, and the lack of drums on tracks like *Baby Let's Play House*, added up to a Rockabilly dream, a predecessor of rock n' roll, and country based. He became a regular on the *Louisiana Hayride* show, driving the girls crazy, but was turned down by the Grand Ol'Opry… for being too 'black'. He was then known variously as the Hillbilly Cat, and the Tupelo Flash, and his reputation was spreading.

The so-called 'Colonel', Tom Parker, manager of country star Eddie Arnold, took over management of Presley in 1955, bought out his contract with Sun Records for a staggering $35,000, and signed him to the giant RCA Corporation.

The first single under the new deal, was *Heartbreak Hotel*, and it became the first of 149 singles hits throughout his career. The first album, Elvis Rock n' Roll No 1, was an all-time classic, with *Lawdy Miss Clawdy, Money Honey*, and *Shake Rattle and Roll* amongst the titles. It too became No 1, and the first of 92 chart albums.

Because Elvis was the most successful recording artiste of all time, his career is worth a final analysis. In the 21st century, you may look back and ask, why? Why did it happen? To simplify, you must look at the basics. Presley's voice was quite unique, drawing from black and white influences, far more than Johnnie Ray or Bill Haley. His looks were outstanding, and 'of the moment', plus he was in the right place at the right time. When Johnnie Ray sang *Such A Night*, it sounded like show business: when Presley sang *One Night*, it sounded like sex on a vinyl plate. But surely, most of all, he had that 'it' quality, the thing you can't tie down. It's as if he was 'meant' to happen; to become the voice of a new generation. Even after death, Presley is still with us, in TV commercials, look-a-like contests, and re-mixed records. He was the great folk hero of the 20th century, no more no less. To dwell on his sad end is best left to biographers. He was simply a phenomenon in life and in death.

Elvis was said to have been frozen out of his own life, declared officially dead, and reduced to Presley look-a-like contests, where he never came better than third.

David Ambrose, *Hollywood Lies*

Despite the cynicism, Elvis Presley was and always will be, the King of rock and roll, and an icon of the 20th century.

There were of course, many other rock legends in the making by the mid-50s. Chuck Berry had appeared at the Newport Jazz Festival, much to the consternation of purist jazz fans, singing *Sweet Little Sixteen*. Little Richard was tearing up theatres with self-penned numbers like *Tutti Frutti,* and Fats Domino, the New Orleans R&B singer, was writing great songs like *Ain't That A Shame*.

As we have already seen, they all had a problem: their colour. Strangely this did not apply to jazz musicians, or at least it seemed not to. Perhaps this was because jazz had been in the mainstream for over thirty years, and was thus regarded as mature and intelligent. This new music, this rock n' roll, could directly affect the morals of white American kids, or at least that was the theory put about by the puritans. Then, like a knight on a white charger, their hero appeared: Pat Boone. A more unlikely rock singer is hard to imagine. Boone was a practicing Baptist, and a college graduate, with a high moral tone! He could certainly sing, and ballads such as *I'll Be Home*, were huge hits. It was when he started to 'cover' black R&B songs that bells started ringing, at least for the younger generation. He sang, properly, *Long Tall Sally, Tutti Frutti*, and *Ain't That A Shame*, eclipsing the originals. The sexual innuendos in these songs escaped him entirely, and in any case, the way he sang them made each song as anodyne as a nursery rhyme. Regardless of this, they were all massive hits, and middle class America was safe; or at least they were, until the kids bought the originals and found true heaven. Here was the start of the real rock rebellion. As if Elvis wasn't enough, now parents had to contend with what they thought of as 'jungle music'; and the more they protested, the more their kids loved it. This new music was 'theirs', and only they could understand it. This was the generation gap, in all its glory.

Of course other white acts, aside from Presley, had that 'something special'. Jerry Lee Lewis drove kids wild, as did Gene Vincent, but one new star somehow bridged the divide, and that I think, was the source of his enormous longevity, in music terms.

Buddy Holly, a young Texan, wrote songs that ultimately resonated with young and old alike. His music was rock based certainly, but it wasn't really 'dangerous'. It was accessible, instant, and somehow 'folksy'.

Everyday was a great teenage love song, with neither the saccharine Pat Boone influence, nor the suggestive rhythm and blues innuendos. It was pure pop. Holly's career lasted less than 18 months, cut short by his death in 1959. Its length is not commensurate with his immense popularity to the present day. He was one of the seminal influences on 20th century popular music, alongside Armstrong, Sinatra and Presley. There is a case to be made that he is possibly one of the greatest, bearing in mind that he wrote all his songs, unlike many of his peers. Besides, as far as rock and roll was concerned, he 'kept the faith'; he died young.

As did his black counterpart Sam Cooke, a writer of pure pop, with a soul edge. Between them, these two men achieved something that had been brewing for a century: the perfect musical crossover of rock, country, soul and blues; black and white harmony.

The more keen eyed amongst you will have noticed that I referred to Presley as a folk hero and to Holly as being folksy. This does not relate to their music in either case, but to their general appeal to the public. If, however, the word 'folk' means appealing to the public, or the common man, why, you may ask, does the actual music that bears the name not do so? Or at least on a larger scale than it appears to?

The answer to this is, it does; or rather, it did (in record sales terms).

Pete Seeger, ex Almanac member, had put together a new group in the late 1940s. In 1950, the Weavers hit the top of the American charts with *Goodnight Irene*, and stayed there for 13 weeks. The song was written by Leadbelly, ex-convict and now folk/blues performer in his own right. The Weavers had other hits with Leadbelly and Woody Guthrie songs, and Pete Seeger's influence stretched into the 1960's folk revival; but Pete had one big problem, his political orientation.

The McCarthy Commission blacklisted him, and his family was attacked by a right wing mob in the Appalachians. He had actually quit the American Communist party in 1951, but he remained tarnished to those in powerful places. Even recording a black convict's song seemed to go against him. *Billboard*, the American music trade paper, even refused to list Weaver hits in their chart, despite qualifying sales. How un-American was that?

Folk has always been the music of the people, and consequently the opiate of the masses, be it communism or socialism, has always had an affiliation. Folk is, and should be, the voice of protest. But folk is also history, a fact overlooked by educationalists and governments, when the teaching of folk heritage songs was discontinued in British primary schools over 20 years ago. Despite 1950s bigotry, this practice continues in the USA, and ensures their children have some idea of their musical background. Sadly, most of that background comes from these islands; and our children are ignorant of the fact through no fault of their own. They have been denied their musical heritage in favour of crass multi-culturalism and political correctness.

Country music and folk were close relatives, and during the 1950s country continued to prosper, helped by a proliferation of cowboy movies, and far more professional record production. Marty Robbins and Ferlin Husky were the big names, but a couple of new ones were coming up fast: Johnny Cash and Jim Reeves. The secret for all of them, was to 'crossover' into the much bigger pop market. None achieved greater success in the 1950s than the Everly Brothers, Don and Phil.

Meanwhile, Hollywood had decided to toy with the new teenage sensations. They had no problem with juvenile delinquents, they made great movie subjects, but the music was something else. The big studio heads were arbiters of public taste and morals, who had been making musicals for years, usually with nowhere storylines, and semi-operatic scores, performed by Mario Lanza and Gordon McCrae. Now they were confused. None of them understood what rock n' roll was all about, but they realised they had to be seen to join the party. The answer? A dirt cheap movie, with a nowhere plot, and instead of Lanza, Bill Haley and his Comets. Brilliant!

The result was a black and white movie, *Rock Around The Clock*, released in 1956. They say it cost $450,000. If that's so, then there was some really creative accountancy going on somewhere. It looked cheap, and therefore it was: but perhaps that was its secret. Kids thought it represented them, and in some cases acted appropriately by smashing up the cinemas to show their approval. The movie moguls realised that their worst fears had been founded, and promptly made a series of rock movies that got progressively worse, except for one.

The Girl Can't Help It was different. To begin with it starred a couple of good actors, Tom Ewell and Edmund O'Brian, plus the improbably endowed Jayne Mansfield. The script was funny, it was in technicolour, and the kids got Gene Vincent, Eddie Cochran, and Little Richard as a bonus. It was probably the best rock n' roll movie ever made. The studio recognised this, and promptly dropped the idea of making anymore,

Hollywood didn't need to worry; they had signed Elvis. Between them and Colonel Parker, they had no difficulty in ruining a raw exciting talent. You can follow the sorry tale of Elvis's movies precisely. The only films of any consequence were made in the 1950s: *Love Me Tender* (based on the 18th century song *Aura Lee*), *Lovin' You* (written by Leiber & Stoller courtesy Tin Pan Alley), *Jailhouse Rock* (written by Leiber & Stoller), and *King Creole* (book by Harold Robbins, music by, yes, you guessed, Leiber & Whatsisname). After that, well it was all downhill: a ghastly succession of bad, forgettable films with Elvis as a racing driver, fishing boat captain, or circus roustabout, with equally forgettable music written largely by... oh dear, they'd 'gone off' too! It's sad what money can do to talent. But I guess it beats starving.

Hollywood and Broadway still had the good old musicals or Rodgers and Hammerstein II, and Lerner and Lowe, and these kept the 'grown ups' happy. The last musical of the 1950s was a very different animal.

West Side Story was a work of genius in every way, not least the amazing timing. Take a classic Shakespearean story, *Romeo & Juliet*, change the setting to 1950s New York, base the characters on the teenage gangs of the city, and what have you got? A hit. Leonard Bernstein's music was so eclectic. It took in rock n'roll, Puerto Rican 'latino' music, and big show songs. It was a wonderful way to end an exciting decade, musically, and for my money, it is one of the greatest musicals ever written, if not the greatest.

Black pop music in America was at a crossroads by 1959. Gospel had helped to influence rhythm and blues: the blues itself was too basic and dirty for mass consumption, and black rock n' rollers were eclipsed by their white counterparts. In effect black music split in half that year, as a new company was formed in Detroit called Tamla Motown, a company that was exclusively black, run by Berry Gordy, writer and producer, with a mission to develop black artistes for the mass (white) market place, and to make some of them superstars. The other 'half' of black music remained embedded in its roots. Soul music would always retain the flavour of the Mississippi Delta, and would nearly always rely on a harmonious blend of black and white influences to keep its diversity alive. The two 'founding fathers' of soul were Sam Cooke and James Brown.

That same year, rock n' roll, the real thing, died. Elvis was in the army, Buddy Holly had died, and the record companies had homogenized an exciting music form to the point of extinction. Fabian and Frankie Avalon were unworthy successors to Elvis & Co. Some thought differently, like John Crosby, the most influential American TV and radio journalist in the 1950s:

Elvis Presley is an unspeakably, untalented young entertainer. This 'abberation' might herald the end of rock n' roll and a return to musical sanity. I mean, where do you go to from Elvis, short of open obscenity, which is against the law. Popular music has been in a tailspin for years now, and I have hopes that with Presley, it has touched bottom, and will just have to start getting better.
John Crosby, journalist, 1956.

I wonder what ever happened to John? We don't know, and we certainly don't care, because like many others he misread the youth movement of the 1950s. So many things changed in that decade as young people gained a greater measure of independence, which had previously been unthinkable, not to mention impossible. This independence covered a host of things, not least fashion, films and music: but music was the catalyst.

Teenagers copied the styles of their favourite stars, and the entertainment and fashion companies began to realise that this new market was valuable, and renewable, every few years. Furthermore their requirements were not so exacting as the old adult markets. They might not always go for rubbish, but you could certainly feed them plastic most of the time.

The other thing the critics of 1950s musical tastes ignored, was the age of the up and coming entrepreneurs, writers and producers. Leiber & Stoller were in their early twenties whilst writing for Presley. The heads of the new thrusting independent record labels were of a similar age. The world was changing but the old guard did not want to hand over the reins. They never had before and they weren't going to start now. Or at least that's what they thought.

11

I Know Where I'm Going

BRITAIN - 1950s.

I guess it was the contrast between our vision of American life, provided by Hollywood, and the drab, black and grey world provided by post-war Europe that made the early 1950s so memorable. Our food was still rationed, while the Americans were buying Oldsmobiles and cheeseburgers! What hope was there, especially if you were young?

Sure, in Britain we had the Ted Heath band, but they were still rooted, or at least appeared to be, in 1940s big band music. We had singers, but Denis Lotis, Lita Roza, and the Stargazers, were pale imitations of the real 'American' thing. And in any case, this was music for a 'cast-off' generation, as far as youth was concerned. At the other end of the market, we had truly dreadful British pop provided by radio stars of the day like Max Bygraves. Who can forget such mind-numbing songs as *Pink Toothbrush*, or *Close The Door, They're Coming In The Window*?

> *You're a pink toothbrush, I'm a blue toothbrush,*
> *Have we met somewhere before?*
> *You're a pink toothbrush, and I think toothbrush,*
> *That we met by the bathroom door*
>   The Pink Toothbrush Song

Now I realise that some of you imagine this to be a children's song, but in truth it was, like many others, aimed squarely (in both senses of the word), at the mainstream pop market. Remember, Britain at this time had no national music radio station, and television was still in its infancy. What this amounted to was pop cultural starvation, and downright, bloody boredom.

Gracie Fields (above)
and Billie Holliday

Frank Sinatra

Mahalia Jackson

Louis Jordan

Hank Williams

Shake, Rattle & Roll
See You Later Alligator   Rock Around The Clock
The Saints Rock & Roll   Rip It Up

*Elvis Presley, Bill Black, Scotty Moore, and Sam Phillips
at Sun Records in 1954*

Chuck Berry

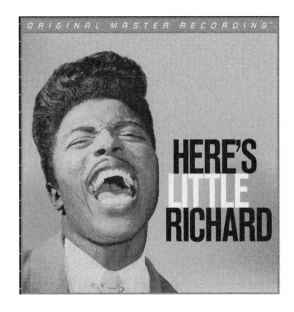

Buddy Holly

Pete Seeger

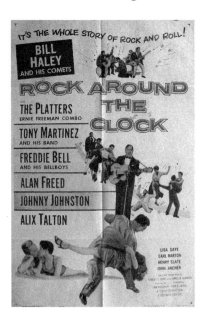

West Side Story

LONNIE DONEGAN
The King Of Skiffle

BRITISH INVASION
SKIFFLE

BBC TV Six-Five Special

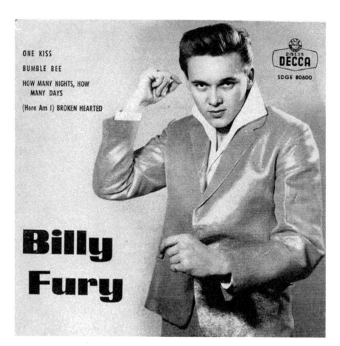

Billy Fury

The summer of love - 1967

Woodstock 1968

Jimi Hendrix (left) and Joan Baez

Sex Pistols

Ziggy Stardust

Elton John   *Whitney Houston*

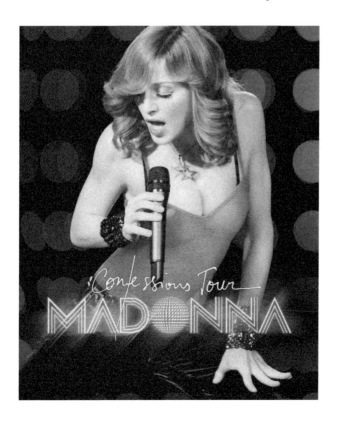

Stevie Wonder

The Springfields (Mike Hurst on the left)

The British record chart (top 12 only), was published for the first time in November 1952, and in its first year every number one was by an American performer, bar four: The Stargazers, Lita Roza, Mantovani and David Whitfield, all, excepting Mantovani, with American songs, and let's face it, he was a 'palm court' orchestra leader. The following year things had improved slightly: there were six, the last being *Let's Have Another Party* by Winifred Atwell, a pianist who sounded as if she belonged in the Red Lion pub circa 1942. Things were not good at home.

In Britain, we were poor cousins as far as entertainment was concerned. In 1954, rock n' roll was merely a whisper from across the ocean; a newspaper article mentioning someone called Elvis who apparently swivelled his hips. Here, we listened to Dicky Valentine, a good, but unexciting band singer trying to sound American. Radio consisted of *The Billy Cotton Bandshow*, desperately mired in a long gone wartime Britain. The only light on an otherwise dim radio dial was Radio Luxembourg. They played American chart music, and if you were lucky enough to have a crystal set (please remember, transistors were not available!), you could get the faint echoes of a new tomorrow.

Not that the old school had disappeared, far from it. The Tony Bennetts, Rosemary Clooneys and Frankie Laines were still going, just. At first they must have been confused, but by 1955, they were terrified. They were the wrong sound, and even worse, the wrong age. They tried to compete (like Perry Como's attempt at rock with *Juke Box Baby*), but it all fell flat. In the UK, similar stars like Dickie Valentine and Alma Cogan were going through the same motions. They had to, they had been brought up in British theatre and music hall, and they were still copying their American counterparts. But you only had to look at youth on British streets to see that something was happening. Teenagers in Edwardian clothes, drape jackets and drainpipe trousers, were everywhere. The Teddy Boys. It was a badge of distinction, along with the DA (duck's arse) hair cut. This was all a million miles away from the comfort of *Worker's Playtime* and *Family Favourites* on BBC Radio.

So, was Britain finished, musically? Decca Records UK hoped not, and signed an ex-merchant seaman, Tommy Hicks. He became Tommy Steele and was our first answer to Elvis. What a hope. He was talented, in a loveable pre-50s cockney kind of way, but it ended there. His first single, *Rock With The Cavemen*, was pretty appalling, but it was a hit:

> *Rock with the cavemen, roll with the cavemen*
> *Stalactite, stalagmite,*
> *Hold your baby very tight,*
> *Rock With The Cavemen*

Tommy had quite a few hits in the UK, and Britain took him to their hearts. But his pop career was short, and he finally moved across to stage and screen musical roles. The odd thing is, he appears to be a non person; the rock encyclopaedias tend to leave him out completely, which seems a little unfair. By 1958, the adjective thing had got out of control with Johnny Gentle, Duffy Power, Vince Eager, Billy Fury etc. It was actually 'amateur night at the Palais', as managers and record companies in the UK attempted to find their new feet.

All through the 1950s, Britain was playing 'catch up' in the record business, which mostly meant copying America. As if to prove the point, we seemed to discover Dixieland jazz again, 40 years after the event, calling it quaintly, Trad, dad. Even this little mixture of cockney rhyming slang and American jive talk (daddy-o), shows the inevitable middle class bias. Jazzers even wore cardigans and smoked pipes! They were cool, just like Bing Crosby in the 1930s. British musicians like Humphrey Lyttelton, Chris Barber, and Ken Colyer, were in the vanguard, and Humph and Colyer fronted their own jazz clubs in London. Old fashioned maybe, but one thing the clubs did, was to present American blues and gospel artists in Britain for the first time. I saw Sonny Terry and Brownie McGhee, Sister Rosetta Tharpe, and Odetta in the late 50s, and my contemporaries like Clapton and Jagger, enjoyed similar experiences, which encouraged them to join the blues movement of the 1960s. But 'trad' musicians and fans saw themselves as a bulwark against the cheap new rock n' roll sounds.

They refused to acknowledge that the origins of jazz and blues came from the same cheap basic roots, and were trapped in a past that seemed to have no desire to examine the future. Lyttelton, for example, only had one hit single, *Bad Penny Blues.* The recording engineer, one Joe Meek, pushed up the level of the drums on the track; too far in Humph's opinion. With the record in the UK charts, he failed to see that this was the disc's main attraction! He wasn't the only one who was blind to what was going on:

After years of tawdry revues, music hall has stumbled on a crock of gold. A small crock admittedly, for in a year or two rock and roll will be as passé as Clara Bow [silent movie actress]. To ask a grown up musician to discuss such music is like asking an epicure to compose a sonnet about bread and water. The new musical rash is so devoid of aesthetic content that there is nothing left to say except that it is a silly noise, and leave it at that.
Benny Green, musician and music critic, 1956

From the Chris Barber jazz band there emerged another important development, by accident. At the end of a recording session for Decca, there was a half hour remaining, and the band had nothing else to record. Barber suggested his banjo player, Lonnie Donegan, could fill in with a couple of blues inspired tunes he had worked on. One of them was *Rock Island Line*, an old traditional song that Leadbelly had breathed new life into. The result was a huge hit for Lonnie in the States, and the accolade of being the creator of a new craze called Skiffle. Actually, it was an old craze, from Chicago in the 1930's, and it simply referred to DIY music, played at house parties on tea chest basses, guitars and banjos, and 'jug blowing'; and that was the strength of the 'new' skiffle. Anyone could do it, after only a few days practice.

Nevertheless, Lonnie took the plaudits, and rightly so. Apart from a stack of hit records, admittedly mostly old traditional tunes, he did more to encourage British youth to pick up the guitar than anyone else, and in a sense helped to create the 1960s music boom. Gibson and Hofner guitars owe an awfully big debt to Mr. Donegan.

Skiffle was sniffed at by jazzers, so youth's alternative to the jazz clubs, was the coffee bar. These could be found mostly in London, the most famous being the 2-I's, in Soho, where Tommy Steele had been discovered. Other young musicians gathered there to play and listen to the new 'skiffle' music. Some of the teenagers customers, drinking coffee and the heady atmosphere of musical freedom, would become the stars of the first wave of British rock and roll. Most of them are long forgotten, but one became the longest running legend of British pop, Cliff Richard.

The arrival of Britain's first West Indian immigrants in the early 1950s, heralded the development of a different branch of pop music. Actually, it heralded several. An American, Harry Belafonte, who had lived in Jamaica for five years, brought 'calypso' to the American and British charts.

The calypso could be either a sweet, gentle West Indian ballad, or it could turn into a funny, streetwise commentary on all things from politics to your mother-in-law. The new Britons brought calypso into the mainstream, and also introduced two other, more upbeat music forms, Ska and Bluebeat. Both had a lazy swing feel, with the emphasis on the second and fourth beats of a 4/4 bar. Strangely the black South Africans also came up with a similar style they called Kwela, but with a little more jazz influence. These early immigrant musical roots would pave the way for Reggae in the late 1960s

As for the record companies, one man stands out from all the rest. Edward Lewis, the founder and Chairman of the British Decca Record Company, was, as far as I am concerned, one of the two godfathers of British pop, and a man who changed the music we listened to.

In Lewis's case, he was a stockbroker who had saved the Decca company, and then taken it over in the 20's. He wore a bowler hat, three-piece suit, and was a scion of society. To teenagers and early rock fans he would have been an anathema. How wrong they would have been. Lewis needed to put Decca on the map after a succession of bad figures through the post-war years. He knew the American scene was alive and vibrant, and hopped on a plane, not so easy in 1955, to the States and toured the country, stopping off at music hot spots. Picture if you can, a delicious image of Lewis in his bowler, with a furled umbrella, sitting with rough hard-nosed American businessmen, and persuading them to release their product in Britain through Decca. Not that they needed much persuasion: no one over here was prepared to release them anyway, until Edward Lewis came along. The result was incredible. Lewis signed labels like Cadence, Roulette, Dot, Atlantic and Chess, and formed a new label called London American to release them in the UK. He then sat back and waited for results. How could he fail? A couple of trips to America netted him all the future rock n' roll greats: Chuck Berry, Little Richard, Fats Domino, Jerry Lee Lewis, Ricky Nelson, the Everly Brothers, Buddy Holly, and through his RCA deal, Elvis!

Not bad for someone more at home at the Ritz than Nick's Diner! His next bright idea was to buy time on Radio Luxembourg. Not advertising slots, but whole programmes. This was unique: a half hour show, paid for by a record company, and playing only the releases from that company, Decca.

Lewis had also been at the forefront of the Long Playing record, an American innovation, although honours for the first releases in the UK, went to EMI. However, he also helped to standardise the new stereophonic sound, and market the unbreakable 45 rpm record. You have to take your hat off to him. I did when I got to know him in the 1960s when he had become Sir Edward, deservedly so.

I mentioned two godfathers. The other was a young TV director called Jack Good. Jack was aware of *American Bandstand,* a music TV show which started its long life in 1952, and he was determined to emulate it in Britain. He got his chance, when the BBC commissioned a music show to be called *Six-Five Special,* and appointed Good as producer/director. What he had to work with was somewhat limited, but then this was the BBC. The first show in February 1957, starred Tommy Steele, Lonnie Donegan and Humphrey Lyttelton. The presenters were not adventurous, just very BBC. Josephine Douglas almost wore twin set and pearls, and Pete Murray actually did wear a cravat, an RAF one at that! No, this wasn't rock n' roll, but at least it was a first attempt at teenage television.

Jack knew his BBC limitations, and he also knew he had an alternative, with the fledgling commercial television network. He produced two pilot shows for ABC TV in May 1958 of a new teen music show. *Oh Boy!* was a long way from *Six-Five Special.* Its style was far more American, and thus punchier and brighter. The show featured a resident big band, still a little 'BBC', called Lord Rockingham's XI, and regulars like Marty Wilde and the Dallas Boys, just a little 'rock n' roll', and a female organist, Cherry Wainer, definitely a little 'Butlin's Holiday Camp'. What it became was a milestone in British pop culture. I even auditioned for the show aged 15. Jack told me to come back when my voice had broken properly! Well, it was a start.

The first ever appearance of Cliff Richard on the *Oh Boy!* show, is still vividly in my memory. The song, *Move It,* was the unintentional single. This was because the record company, EMI, preferred the other side, *Schoolboy Crush*, a slushy ballad. Jack Good saw the potential in Cliff's image, and suggested the 'B' side, *Move It*, would make better television.

I saw it, along with millions of other teenagers, and I was spellbound. It wasn't Elvis, but it was our very own greasy hair, curled lip, drape jacket, and best of all, driving rock n' roll guitar. That was it; home-grown rock had arrived, at least for a short time. Cliff would never again make such a perfect homage to rock n' roll, despite trying.

Jack Goode's influence continued, as he brought over American stars, to be seen for the first time on British TV. The result was that some, like Eddie Cochran and Gene Vincent, became more popular in Britain than their own country, and in some cases even ended up living here.

The 1950s in Britain was a time of discovery for teenagers. Inspired by rock n' roll, or its heroes, the fashion industry began to take a small interest. A street in London's West End called Foubert's Place became the first place a young man could buy red or green cord shirts! And they measured your inside leg for the same price. Tapered cords and jeans were also available at Vince Man's Shop and Adonis. Foubert's Place is just off another larger thoroughfare, Carnaby Street.

Television had arrived big-time, with the Coronation of 1953, and the first programmes aimed directly at teenagers followed soon after. Lonnie Donegan had made the guitar an instrument of desire for thousands of young hopefuls, and even though we were still copying our American cousins, the next generation would reap the real dividend.

We were catching up with the Americans, which was amazing since we only really started trying in 1955. In less than ten years Britain would be out of sight and swinging.

12

Land Of Hope And Glory

I don't intend to dwell heavily on the amazing changes in popular music from the 1960s to the present day. This has been covered extensively in many other books, some good, some indifferent. But it is a period everyone, even those who were not there, thinks they know. I will not disabuse you, for to do so would be impolite and result in a book twice as heavy as this one! Suffice to say that even when I look back to the summers of love, the sun always appeared to be shining, which it wasn't. On such imperfect memories, legends are perpetuated.

Black music had come of age with the creation of the first black mainstream record company. Tamla Motown, founded by Berry Gordy, set out to sell black artists to white audiences. Groups like the Supremes and the Four Tops, were 'schooled' in deportment and performance, and dressed in ball gowns and tuxedos. It was a smart move and it worked, but it was, in a sense, contrived. On the other side of the tracks however, black music stayed true to its roots as Soul music, a combination of blues and secular gospel music, found its voice in the deep South, with the success of James Brown and Otis Redding. Motown however, would become the dominant form of the genre, with two of the greatest black singers of all time, Marvin Gaye and Stevie Wonder.

The first two years of the new decade gave little indication of the musical hurricane gathering strength in Britain. However, there were signs if you cared to look. British politics was about to enter a new phase. The 'old' Tory hierarchy was on the ropes; Suez had seen to that in the mid 50s, and a new scandal was about to erupt that would send shock waves around the country. Soon the names of John Profumo, Christine Keeler and Stephen Ward would usher in a new permissive era and release the power of frustrated British youth.

By now, real 50s rock n' roll, a music truly <u>discovered</u> by 50s teenagers, had been appropriated by the record companies on both sides of the Atlantic, re-packaged and served up as homogenized youth music; the beginning of a Simon Cowell world! Pretty boys with nice voices were the order of the day, not dissimilar to the *Pop Idol* stars of the 21st century. America had Frankie Avalon and Fabian, while Britain boasted Adam Faith and Cliff Richard. None represented a 'threat', they were squeaky clean, and their songs had more in common with the London Docks than the Mississippi Delta. Even TV producer Jack Good had fallen prey to this sad state of affairs. His new show was called *Boy Meets Girls*, a saccharine version of his mind-blowing 50s show *Oh Boy!* Instead of Marty Wilde regaling us with *Endless Sleep*, a dark, moody rock anthem, we got Jess Conrad singing about his pullover:

> *This pullover that you gave to me*
> *It is lovely, I wear it constantly*

My God, how had it come to this?

It was actually a triumph of visuals over content, inadvertently assisted by the establishments desire to finish off the overtly sexual, aggressively driven rock of the previous decade; the music of youth.

Notable exceptions in Britain were Billy Fury, a young Liverpudlian, firmly in the Elvis mould and smouldering with sex, and a group who looked uncannily like 80s stars Adam and The Ants and Duran Duran. Johnny Kidd and the Pirates may have looked like pantomime characters, but their big hit *Shaking All Over* became one of the great British rock n' roll anthems.

American stars like Eddie Cochran and Gene Vincent also found a new lease of life in the UK, albeit a short one, as Vincent was badly injured in the same crash that killed Eddie on an English road in 1960.

Why was British youth so in thrall to real rock n' roll?

Unlike their American counterparts, British teenagers of the late 1950s were desperately seeking an identity, which rock provided. It is no coincidence that the likes of Buddy Holly, Little Richard and Jerry Lee Lewis were more popular in Britain than the USA, and have remained so to the present day. Even more importantly, the British music scene in the early 60s was like a pressure cooker. Thousand of youngsters who had been influenced by rock in the 50s, who had picked up guitars and copied Lonnie Donegan, Delta blues singers and Elvis, were about to find their own feet and change the course of pop music. Amongst their number were young Clapton, McCartney, Lennon, Richards, and Jagger, to name but a few.

And there was me.

I had been working at Lloyds of London as a trainee broker, just the job for an aspiring rock singer. I understood nothing of insurance, nor did I want to. I divided most of my time between a billiards hall in Lime Street and hiding in the lavatories attempting to write songs. I was introduced to a 'gentleman' broker, who claimed to be a publicist for Cliff Richard, but on reflection appeared to be a dead ringer for Oscar Wilde, right down to the exotically coloured carnations he wore daily! His name was Ray, which would not have endeared him to Lady Bracknell. Ray got me a few gigs at the Shepherds Bush Empire, rock and roll shows on a Saturday afternoon, where everyone looked the same! Black shirts, white shoes and medallions. If the audience liked you, you were safe. Otherwise coins and baked beans cans were hurled indiscriminately... and the cans were full! These shows didn't get me anywhere, but they did give me some useful experience, including how to dodge missiles. My mother, bless her heart, was always on the lookout for opportunities in the music business, and in mid 1961 she answered an ad in *The Stage* newspaper for a 'young singer/ guitarist for well established group'. She never told me, in case there was no response. But there was, and a month later I turned up for an audition at Quaglino's Restaurant in London. I had no idea which group it was, and was none the wiser as I waited my turn. At the back of the club I saw a woman with a beehive blonde hairdo, and thought I recognised her; but I wasn't sure. After the audition, the expected voice said 'thanks, we'll let you know', the standard response. I didn't think I would hear a thing, but I was wrong. A fortnight later, I received a letter from Tom Springfield inviting me to join the Springfields. Within three months I found myself in

Nashville, Tennessee, recording a new album: we (the Springfields) had a top 10 USA single, the first ever by a British vocal group, and our new release in the UK, *Island Of Dreams,* was No. 2 in the charts. Oh, and we were made honorary members of a new band's fan club, the Beatles. John Lennon presented us with our cards on stage at the Cavern. What a way to kick off the 60s!

In October 1962 we were NME poll winners in top group category, with the Beatles as runners up. But the order of things was about to change.

America was pre-occupied with the Cuban missile crisis and the space race. It had a young charismatic President and it had embarked on a war in Vietnam. The assassination of Kennedy in 1963 would leave a huge vacuum in the USA, both culturally and politically. I believe this partially explains the British pop 'invasion' that was about to land on America's shores. The only part of the world that could feed the American music machine was the mother country. It was all about language.

The other reason, obviously, was the desperation of British youth eager to shrug off the greyness of post-war Britain. Add to this the sheer musical energy and innovation of so many young bands waiting to happen, and you can see why England was about to 'swing'.

We knew what was about to happen, and the Springfields broke up in October that year, knowing the writing was on the wall. What happened next was musical fantasy. The Beatles and the Liverpool sound dominated world pop. The secret was the quintessential Englishness of the music. It was almost pure Music Hall. From Ray Davies and the Kinks to the Small Faces, this new pop was not a slave to America. It stood on its own.

I wanted to start a new band and in early 1964 I went looking for potential members. In the Gia-Conda coffee bar in London's Denmark Street, I was introduced to a 17-year-old guitarist called Jimmy Page. He joined up as did another great player, Albert Lee. With the addition of keyboard player Tony Ashton, Mike Hurst and The Methods was born. Just one problem though; we all loved country rock which was totally American. If ever the timing was wrong, this was it. We lasted for six months and split up. England would no longer dance to an American beat. We had our own tunes.

In the USA a young folk singer was making a name for himself. Bob Dylan was a dead ringer for Woody Guthrie, in political and musical style, but instead of the Depression of the 30s, Dylan was writing and singing about the changing times, of nuclear winters, youthful protest and the like. He was actually articulating the rebellion of youth to come, already propounded by 'beat' writers like Jack Kerouac. In the 50s, teenagers had rebelled, in a way, but principally through the music. After all, everything was new and exciting to them, and in an understandable way, juvenile. The protesters then, were the older literary generation like Harold Pinter and Arnold Wesker. Now in this new decade teenagers would really discover their 'causes', and most importantly, they would make themselves heard.

Dylan was not above using Britain's folk heritage when necessary, just like his country cousins in the Appalachians. For example, his song *Girl From The North Country*, when played in a minor rather than major key, is very similar to the 18th century ballad *Scarborough Fair*. Plus ca change! Actually, the folk movement in both the USA and the UK had never gone away. The Springfields were originally a folk group, while in America Peter Paul and Mary, the Kingston Trio and the New Christy Minstrels were still flying the flag. As the 1960s progressed, others emerged like Donovan, a rather whimsical flower child, and Barry McGuire in the States, who articulated the CND movement with his apocryphal *Eve Of Destruction*.

As a record producer (which I now was), I was lucky enough to be at the forefront of the now rapidly expanding British music explosion. Days were spent in recording studios with newcomers like Marc Bolan and a young man called Steven Giorgiou. Steve had changed his name to Cat Stevens, and I signed him up for record production and management. Neither of us ever looked back as we headed for the Summer of Love.

British TV had finally caught up with the music scene, and ATV's *Ready, Steady, Go!* was the show every rock artist wanted to be on. Now was the time that if you were not 'in' you were most definitely out! New British bands vied to appear on RSG, which was their passport to fame and fortune. Viewers had their dreams and most importantly, their identification confirmed by groups like The Who performing *My Generation*, and the phrase 'Hope I die before I get old', which entered the teenage lexicon of life. Who would have thought that many of the same bands would still be performing the same songs 40 years down the road!

What this really meant was that the 60s generation would certainly grow old, but many would <u>never</u> grow up. Youth would be theirs, forever. The effects of such enormous social and cultural changes are still being felt today. Parents, the offspring of the 60s flower children, often see themselves as friends of their own children rather than parents. They can bond and party together, something that would have been anathema before 1963. On the upside, pensioners stay younger longer. Just think of the parents of the 1940s and how old they seemed at the time. My own father, at 60, was an elderly man compared to many of the same age group today.

<u>The</u> summer of love in 1967 was the zenith of the ideals redolent in the 'hippie' generation. By the following year things were going down hill, at least in terms of 'peace and love'. Ban the Bomb marchers were on the world's streets; anti-Vietnam war student demonstrations, largely left wing in political terms, were gaining notoriety in the USA, Britain, and Europe. You could say that all of these were clear manifestations of a desire for peace. However, such events often turned into bloody and dangerous confrontation, thereby diminishing their very existence.

Popular music didn't just blindly aid and abet these movements, but to some extent naively articulated them to an equally naive audience. Not that there is anything wrong with 'peace and love' as a genuine life style, but rather to make the point that aspiration for the many can sometimes be confused with manipulation by the few.

Woodstock in 1969 may be viewed as the end of an ideal. Certainly it was the chronological end of an era, but it might also be seen as a spiritual end. Half a million young people coming together to save the world, their world; but not having the foggiest idea of how this could be achieved other than by making love in public and attacking a faceless establishment. The events that closely followed Woodstock seemed to presage the closing chapter of the 'swinging 60s'. The Hollywood murders of Sharon Tate and friends by the

Charles Manson gang, and the killing of a young girl at the Rolling Stones Altemont concert that same year sounded a death knell for the hippie culture, and made it quite obvious that half a million young people could not change the world, and that music simply reflects society; it does not change it.

Before we leave the 1960s, we should look at another strange anomaly in music that reflected attitudes to racial divides. The decade began with Civil Rights marches, and the dreams of Martin Luther King. By the close of the 60s, these dreams were a lot closer to reality, helped in some small measure by the music; or rather the singers.

Back in the 50s Elvis and some others had appropriated the sounds of black blues singers, but by the close of the 60s more and more singers adopted a black sound! Dusty Springfield was referred to as the White Negress. The upcoming heavy rock bands, had screaming lead singers who had much more in common with Howlin' Wolf than the early Beatles. This trend did not dominate completely as we moved into the 70s. The early part of that decade was the time of the great singer/songwriters; James Taylor, Carly Simon, Carole King and Paul Simon et al. These performers used the English language to good purpose, and filled the same role as the minstrels of the Middle Ages; they were communicators. However, the strict 'pop' market was in disarray. For lack of originality, a crop of groups showed up who looked and played like the old 50s rock groups, and often, like Showaddywaddy, even used the same songs. Mark you, the audience was now younger, in the lower teens. Then, with the appearance of the Jackson Five and the Osmonds (both family bands, one white, one black), the record buyers became younger still; ten to twelve year olds. Their parents, the teenagers of the swinging 60s, were buying them records and (confusingly) taking them to what were now being called 'teeny bopper' concerts. Older teenagers, mostly girls, were consoled by the likes of David Cassidy, who had been created by a TV series, *The Partridge Family* in the USA. Real music buffs sought out new upcoming bands like Queen, ELO, 10CC and in America, the Eagles and Chicago, or went to see the new Stadium rock bands, Zeppelin and Purple. But this was 'grown up' music, which 60s parents could really relate to and who in turn introduced them to their older children. Popular music was fragmenting and so was its audience.

None of these music styles really captured a moment; a zeitgeist, and they were non-representative of a large swathe of teenagers who still wanted to rebel...in some shape or form. At the very least, to have a music that was theirs, not their parents'. To a certain extent, a new neo-Gothic style of heavy rock called Metal fitted the bill. Bands like Iron Maiden and Motorhead brought the idea of 'devil worship' to the table, though in reality everyone knew these guys were simply re-visiting the early days of Saxons and Celts and turning them into show business! Likewise Reggae, an off-shoot of Ska and Bluebeat, had its following, largely through the songwriting and performance talents of Bob Marley. Just as with rock n' roll, this was a black and white affair, for without the belief and business acumen of white Jamaican Chris Blackwell, owner of Island Records, Marley might have struggled. In the early 70s an American band called The Ramones was exhibiting a rough aggressive new type of music. It was crude and unapologetic, as its name suggested. Punk was a trans-Atlantic development and it was everything a young rebel could want: a style of clothing, haircuts and attitudes that sent shock waves through the establishment and general adult population. The Sex Pistols should perhaps be viewed as a brilliant marketing concept, conceived by a smart London boy Malcolm McClaren, rather than the leaders of an organic movement. Bands like The Clash, The Damned and The Cure were closer to the mark, musically and politically. The essence of Punk was a desire to change society through anarchy. It was possibly the last true voice of teenage rebellion.

Record companies, ever eager to maximise their buying public, looked for something that had a broader appeal than Punk, and found it in Disco. Helped by the movie *Saturday Night Fever* and the exploding club scene in New York, Disco became the dance craze of the 70s. It was also the last time that a dance style dominated pop culture. Disco was not organic however, and was synthesised in all sense of the word. Not only were synthesiser keyboards de rigeur, but the actual number of beats to the bar were carefully studied and calibrated to suit non-stop 'getting down and dirty'. The Bee Gees, a hirsute 'falsetto to the fore' band, were the inspiration for all would be John Travoltas. An odd bunch from the 60s, they probably ended up writing more hits than anyone else, except possibly the Beatles!

By the mid 1970s a new clutch of singer songwriters from both sides of the Atlantic, were making their presence felt. Elton John, an unlikely figure from Pinner in Middlesex, had taken America by storm, and another equally unlikely soul, David Bowie, who had started out singing about a 'Laughing Gnome', re-invented himself several times, the most successful being Ziggy Stardust. In the States, Bruce Springsteen and Billy Joel sang about America, and became icons worldwide. Sad to reflect that these great performers and writers, were probably the last great artists of the 20th century, and we are still waiting for their like to appear in the 21st!

At the close of the 70s a new music emerged from the black ghettos of Los Angeles. I use the term 'music' advisedly, since there was little or no evidence of tunes. Rap and it dancing cousin Hip Hop, was the voice of disaffected black American youth. It was also the ultimate in teenage musical rebellion. There were no melodies, and few lyrics that could be understood by anyone over 30. You couldn't whistle tracks by Grandmaster Flash or the Sugar Hill Gang, but you could dance to them, and that dance music would be the prevailing club soundtrack for the next quarter of a century.

Video had been commercially available since the mid-70s, via the good old Philips VCR machines, but it had been unwieldy and unreliable. Now, as the 80s dawned the preferred system was the VHS recorder, and lo, MTV was born in 1982. The music video was the most exciting thing to happen to pop for a generation, and the record companies embraced it enthusiastically, even seeing it originally, as a money-spinner. MTV would have to pay for each showing, wouldn't they? Not for long as it turned out. The power lay with the broadcaster, and within a few years the record companies were giving videos to MTV; videos which were costing them enormous sums of money. But hey, the artists were paying in the end, so that was alright wasn't it? Yes, but only as long as sales continued to grow, which was surely guaranteed. Oops! In Britain, the prevailing 80s music trends utilised the MTV generation perfectly, and in a very British way. The New Romantics were so utterly British and eccentric. ABC, Spandau Ballet and Duran Duran were all perfect for the times. Their outlandish costumes, and faux 'Englishness' were exactly what the MTV doctor ordered. The songs were another matter. Harmless and often tuneful they might have been, but they were not often challenging. Think Boy George, and while we are on that subject, think sexual orientation. The New Romantics portrayed a sexual ambivalence, but it was obvious that homosexuality was now regarded in a much more

111

acceptable light than in previous times, and some of the music articulated this awareness in no uncertain terms. Frankie Goes To Hollywood shot to number one with the graphically sexual song *Relax*. It didn't phase the younger generation, and indeed one must say the older generation appeared blissfully unaware of the lyrical content. National radio, the BBC, who had banned rock n' roll in the 50s and various other songs through the years that they thought 'unsuitable' for listeners, seemed almost enlightened as they played *Relax* to death. My belief is they really had no idea what it was about! You can surely see the fun in all this. Older generations who had been referring to homosexuals as 'queers' and 'homos' all their lives, were now boogying furiously at wedding parties to a song extolling a gay life style!

As with homosexuality, feminism also made its mark in the 80s through music. There had always been fantastic female singers and performers, and many had sold a lot of records. But it was not until 1984 that a woman achieved a multi-million selling album, and she was Whitney Houston. The year after came the woman who changed things forever for women in music: Madonna. Not a considerable talent, but a great marketing phenomenon, Madonna gave women the boost they needed to truly make their mark on the music scene, in their own right.

Compilations by many hit artists from the past became big sellers for the record companies, as the new CD format became increasingly popular through the 80s. But what a strange decade it was for music. From the dying embers of Punk, through the New Romantics, to disco, rap and hip hop, and all the re-hashed hits of yesteryear. This was audience fragmentation on a scale not seen before, and what it presaged was not good.

If the 80s had seen big changes and diversity in the music and the record buyer, the 90s would prove a big disappointment... at least to good music lovers. It was the decade of marketing; of hype over substance. One small light at the end of the tunnel was the explosion of Britpop. The biggest of the bands, Oasis, Blur, Pulp and Suede were not bad, but they sometimes laboured under the weight of unoriginality, brought on by trying to combat the artifice of the New Romantics and trying to sound more gritty and real. This only served to make them 60s clones in many cases, albeit good ones. Then came the full horror. The marketing man's dream and the music lover's nightmare: the so-called boy and girl bands. Largely untalented, but lovingly put together by marketing gurus, groups like the Spice Girls, Boyzone and Backstreet Boys dominated the charts. The fact that generally only one of the group ever seemed to be able to sing, whilst the other voices were patently added by real singers, seemed to pass the listening audience by. Why should they care? If the record was to their liking that was sufficient, and the fact that it was often a musical con job was by the way. Take That were one of the few who had a degree of talent, largely because of their songwriter/singer Gary Barlow, who knew the song was all important, and Robbie Williams who for my money was the closest thing to a British pop idol since Cliff Richard .

Finally, towards the end of the 90s the lunatics got their hands on the asylum. Technology and marketing reigned supreme. TV shows like *Pop Idol*, *Fame Academy* and *The X Factor* became the bedrock of new 'talent'. How could this be? Simple. Since the beginning of the internet revolution, young people began to realise that they were being empowered by this new medium and that they no longer needed to be in thrall to major record companies and industry bodies. Now, they could sit at home in their bedrooms, make their own records for next to nothing and then sell them on the web. Easy as that. Then the Simon Cowells of the world also figured out that by using TV as a direct marketing tool, they could sign up their own artists, present them on national TV once a week, then release them on their own labels; and no-one ever bothered to mention the Monopolies Commission! And finally, the big name artist compilations were selling far less. After all, how long are you prepared to go on buying the same product in different formats? Yes, all in all the 90s was a sad decade musically speaking, and the early 'naughties' (as they are called) are not much better. But the changes wrought are now so colossal that the old music industry is unrecognisable from that of the 20th century. It is no longer a question of the singer or the song; it's just marketing, marketing, marketing stupid!

The major record companies, unable to cope with illegal downloads and file sharing, are all but finished. Sales of records are down on average 7% per annum! Downloads, meant to be the way forward, have also not lived up to their potential and the number of new acts looking for a break has risen exponentially. There is no answer to this. It is and was inevitable, and it's called progress.

So, where are we now, musically? Up **** creek without a paddle? Spoilt for choice? Wallowing in nostalgia? Embarrassed by the riches of musical youth? It's probably a little of all these and more, summed up by one word, confusion.

The record industry is dying while there are more new artists than ever trying to 'make it'. The record companies' dwindling reserves are spent on an extraordinary number of 'next big things', viz Newton Faulkner, Paulo Nettini, Jack Johnson, Jamie Fox, Josh Grogan, Duffy, James Blunt, Dido, Katie Mellua, Nerina Pallot, KT Tunstall, Daniel and Natasha Bedingfield, Tom Baxter, the Hoosiers, Arcade Fire, the Zutons, Rianna, Lili Allen, Amy Winehouse, the list is endless. Some have had great success, many will struggle, but will any of their names or any of their music last as long as say, David Bowie, Billy Joel, Bob Dylan or James Taylor? Perhaps, but I think it unlikely.

Old artists make spectacular comebacks, which fulfill two important criteria; the (old) fans are convinced their heroes are still the best, and the bands increase their already overweight bank balances. But if we of a certain age are truthful, don't we find some, if not all of them, just a little boring? I love the Eagles, but to see five 60+ year olds sitting on stools, singing beautifully, is not quite enough. The glory and enthusiasm of youth is missing and that's what rock is all about, surely?

Some old heroes have taken on unfamiliar roles. Who would have thought Bob Dylan would turn up as a BBC Radio 2 presenter, and crack corny jokes for two hours!

On the dance/soul/R&B front it's no better. Dizzee Rascal, 50 Cent and Kanye West are no substitute for Marvin Gaye and Otis Redding, but they are of their time, and subsequently peripheral. People have stopped asking when the 'next' Beatles will appear. This is probably becuase we realise that is all but impossible. Why should thousands turn out at Heathrow to welcome home a great British rock success? Its been done, and done at a time when everything was exciting and new. Now we see things for what they always were, but never realised at the time. Nothing is really new; it's all in the presentation. The result is what I call the Tesco effect. We have too much choice. Walk down a supermarket aisle, and a bewildering array of goods assails the senses. I want a packet of

Cheddar cheese, but which shall I choose? There are at least 12 different varieties. Do I buy big carrots, carrots with leaves on, baby carrots, frozen carrots etc? I want a salad, but I can choose from five different lettuces, Mediterranean salad, Thai salad, green/mixed etc. And God help us, it's the same with music, and many of you will say 'why shouldn't it be?' I can't argue with that, the times have changed and the internet has changed the way we view things, buy things and enjoy things, not least music.

The internet has empowered people to a degree unheard of in the last century. However, it has also increased the fragmentation of music buyers and musicians to that same degree. And what of the music itself? Today's stars are as good or bad as their predecessors, and a few are excellent. However, most lack one thing; the song. Today, most artists are only interested in quick money, and the quickest route to it, and the talent shows serve them well. But writing a great song takes effort and above all, love. It also requires an industry that sees this clearly, and that has all but disappeared. It's not the business I fell in love with all those years ago, but surely the music must go on. It's always with us, but until writers start coming up with lyrics like these again, it might just take a while to improve.

> *What is the point of this story?*
> *What information pertains?*
> *The thought that life could be better,*
> *is woven indelibly into our hearts and our brains*
> Paul Simon, *Train In The Distance*

The Author

Mike Hurst's first appearance on stage was at the Metropolitan Theatre, London, at the age of four. As part of a theatre group run by his mother, Flavia, Mike appeared with the great comedians of the day like Max Miller and Sid Field in the dying days of Music Hall. Rumours that Mike was responsible for its demise are untrue.

Mike started playing guitar aged 12 and his first professional rock appearance was singing at the premiere of *Jailhouse Rock* in London in 1958. After the usual coffee bar and local theatre gigs, he auditioned for EMI aged 16, and failed manfully. Undeterred, Mike joined the Springfields alongside Dusty and Tom in 1962, and achieved the first hit USA single ever by a British vocal group, *Silver Threads And Golden Needles*. The Springfields were NME poll winners for the top UK group that same year, with the runners up being the Beatles!

The Springfields broke up at the end of 1963, and Mike put a new group together, called Mike Hurst and the Methods. The name might not have been great, but the band was. His lead guitarist was a 17-year-old Jimmy Page, and his second stringer was Albert Lee, with Tony Ashton on keys. The band played country rock, which was not the flavour of the month! This resulted in the band breaking up at the close of 1964.

By 1965, Mike was a record producer, and he was lucky enough to find Marc Bolan cutting his first single, *The Wizard*. A few months later he met the man who changed his life in business terms, Cat Stevens. Mike produced and managed Cat, and it made Mike's career as a producer. From 1966 to 1985, Mike achieved 53 hit singles and 25 gold and platinum albums with artists like Cat, Manfred Mann, The Move, Spencer Davis, PP Arnold, Showaddywaddy, Shakin' Stevens and many others.

In 1984, Mike put a new group together with Mary Hopkin, called Sundance, and toured with Doctor Hook across the UK, including appearances at Wembley Arena and on the Parkinson show.

In the late 80s and throughout the 90s, Mike and his huge family (wife Marjorie and six children) ran a summer camp for kids at their farm in Devon. He also continued to run theatre groups for children in his home town Henley on Thames and in Devon. In 1999, Mike was awarded a Lifetime Achievement Gold Badge by the British Academy of Songwriters and Composers. He still runs his own band, with old friends Ray Fenwick (ex Ian Gillan Band) and Clem Cattini (ex Tornados). He started a summer residential school for young musicians at Stowe School in 2006, and formed a new company Rockmasters, which is currently being franchised around the country and abroad.

Since 1994, Mike has been lecturing at schools in the UK on the history of popular music from the 16th century to the present day. His family now includes 16 grandchildren. Where he got the time to write this book is a mystery.

Index

THE MUSICMAKERS

A lecture on the history of English speaking popular music

Mike Hurst takes you on a musical journey from the 16th century to the present day; from early minstrels to the Arctic Monkeys. Our folk music from the Middle Ages was transported by the early settlers to the New World, and its echoes can still be heard in Nashville today. The arrival of black African slaves who embraced Christianity and its hymns gave us spirituals and subsequently gospel, soul, rhythm and blues and rap. The syncopation of Ragtime, eastern European immigrants and military bands brought us jazz, rock n' roll and dance music. The Musicmakers is a story rich in history and cultural development, and a story of racial divides coming together in a truly colour-blind medium, music.

The music of the common man is told by one man and a guitar, Mike Hurst. As a member of top 1960s group The Springfields and the successful record producer of Cat Stevens, Marc Bolan, The Four Tops and many others, Mike is more than qualified to give young people the benefit of his lifetime in music.

THE MUSICMAKERS is a must for schools and organisations with an interest in popular music. For more information call Mike Hurst on 01628 475520 or 07815 622272.

For information on Mike Hurst's Rockmasters rock schools see www.rockmasters.net